successful workplace
COMMUNICATION

chartered
management
institute
inspiring leaders

successful workplace
COMMUNICATION

PHIL BAGULEY

HODDER
EDUCATION
PART OF HACHETTE LIVRE UK

The publisher has used its best endeavours to ensure that the URLs for external websites referred to in this book are correct and active at the time of going to press. However, the publisher and the author have no responsibility for the websites and can make no guarantee that a site will remain live or that the content will remain relevant, decent or appropriate.

Orders: Please contact Bookpoint Ltd, 130 Milton Park, Abingdon, Oxon OX14 4SB. Telephone: (44) 01235 827720, Fax: (44) 01235 400454. Lines are open from 9.00 to 5.00, Monday to Saturday, with a 24-hour message answering service. You can also order through our website www.hoddereducation.co.uk.

British Library Cataloguing in Publication Data
A catalogue record for this title is available from the British Library.

ISBN-13: 978 0340 983 898

First published   2009
Impression number   10 9 8 7 6 5 4 3 2 1
Year   2013 2012 2011 2010 2009

Typeset by Transet Limited, Coventry, England.
Printed in Great Britain for Hodder Education, an Hachette UK Company, 338 Euston Road, London NW1 3BH, by CPI Cox & Wyman, Reading, Berkshire RG1 8EX.

Hachette UK's policy is to use papers that are natural, renewable and recyclable products and made from wood grown in sustainable forests. The logging and manufacturing processes are expected to conform to the environmental regulations of the country of origin.

The Chartered Management Institute

The Chartered Management Institute is the only chartered professional body that is dedicated to management and leadership. We are committed to raising the performance of business by championing management.

We represent 71,000 individual managers and have 450 corporate members. Within the Institute there are also a number of distinct specialisms, including the Institute of Business Consulting and Women in Management Network.

We exist to help managers tackle the management challenges they face on a daily basis by raising the standard of management in the UK. We are here to help individuals become better managers and companies develop better managers.

We do this through a wide range of products and services, from practical management checklists to tailored training and qualifications. We produce research on the latest 'hot' management issues, provide a vast array of useful information through our online management information centre, as well as offering consultancy services and career information.

You can access these resources 'off the shelf' or we can provide solutions just for you. Our range of products and services is designed to ensure companies and managers develop their potential and excel. Whether you are at the start of your career or a proven performer in the boardroom, we have something for you.

We engage policy makers and opinion formers and, as the leading authority on management, we are regularly consulted on a range of management issues. Through our in-depth research and regular policy surveys of members, we have a deep understanding of the latest management trends.

For more information visit our website **www.managers.org.uk** or call us on **01536 207307**.

Chartered Manager

Transform the way you work

The Chartered Management Institute's Chartered Manager award is the ultimate accolade for practising professional managers. Designed to transform the way you think about your work and how you add value to your organisation, it is based on demonstrating measurable impact.

This unique award proves your ability to make a real difference in the workplace.

Chartered Manager focuses on the six vital business skills of:

- Leading people
- Managing change
- Meeting customer needs
- Managing information and knowledge
- Managing activities and resources
- Managing yourself

Transform your organisation

There is a clear and well-established link between good management and improved organisational performance. Recognising this, the Chartered Manager scheme requires individuals to demonstrate how they are applying their leadership and change management skills to make significant impact within their organisation.

Transform your career

Whatever career stage a manager is at Chartered Manager will set them apart. Chartered Manager has proven to be a stimulus to career progression, either via recognition by their current employer or through the motivation to move on to more challenging roles with new employers.

But don't take just our word for it …

Chartered Manager has transformed the careers and organisations of managers in all sectors.

- *'Being a Chartered Manager was one of the main contributing factors which led to my recent promotion.'*
  Lloyd Ross, Programme Delivery Manager, British Nuclear Fuels

- *'I am quite sure that a part of the reason for my success in achieving my appointment was due to my Chartered Manager award which provided excellent, independent evidence that I was a high quality manager.'*
  Donaree Marshall, Head of Programme Management Office, Water Service, Belfast

- *'The whole process has been very positive, giving me confidence in my strengths as a manager but also helping me to identify the areas of my skills that I want to develop. I am delighted and proud to have the accolade of Chartered Manager.'*
  Allen Hudson, School Support Services Manager, Dudley Metropolitan County Council

- *'As we are in a time of profound change, I believe that I have, as a result of my change management skills, been able to provide leadership to my staff. Indeed, I took over three teams and carefully built an integrated team, which is beginning to perform really well. I believe that the process I went through to gain Chartered Manager status assisted me in achieving this and consequently was of considerable benefit to my organisation.'*
  George Smart, SPO and D/Head of Resettlement, HM Prison Swaleside

To find out more or to request further information please visit our website **www.managers.org.uk/cmgr** or call us on **01536 207429**.

Contents

Preface   xvii

CHAPTER 01

WHAT'S IT ALL ABOUT?   1
Communication – why and when   1
Communication in the workplace   2
What is communication?   3
One-way or two-way?   6
Communication channels and noise   8
Effective workplace communication   11
The three golden rules   11
Who are you communicating with?   12
What do you communicate?   12
How do you communicate?   15
Communication difficulties   17
Summary   19

CHAPTER 02

ARE YOU LISTENING?   21
Can you hear me?   21
Listening and hearing   23

Why listen?   26
First steps to effective listening   27
How to listen effectively   30
Ways and means   33
Summary   38

CHAPTER 03

WHY DIDN'T HE (OR SHE) SMILE?   41
Bodily communication   41
The science of body language   44
Gestures   46
Facial expressions   47
Gaze   48
Touching   49
Using space   50
Posture   51
Appearance   52
How to use body language   54
Summary   56

CHAPTER 04

HOW WOULD YOU LIKE TO ...?   59

Persuasion   59
The influence spectrum   60
Persuasion – straight or twisted?   62
The four fundamentals   63
The where and why of persuasion   64
Persuasive overtures   66
One to one   66
Organisational persuasion   69
Money, money, money   71
Goals and glory   72
Compatibility   72
Summary   73

CHAPTER 05

DO YOU WANT TO DO A DEAL?   77

Negotiations in the workplace   77
Conflict, conflict and conflict   79
Conflict resolution   80
What is negotiation?   81

How do you negotiate? 82

The bargaining zone 87

Negotiating – do's and dont's 88

Summary 93

CHAPTER 06

CAN I EXPLAIN? 95

Explaining – the what and why 95

Explaining – a definition 97

Explaining – the ways and means 98

Talk 99

Written material 102

Presentations 103

Summary 112

CHAPTER 07

WRITE WORDS OR WRONG WAYS? 115

The written word 115

Written material and spoken words 117

What and where? 119

Paper and ink 120

Planning 121

Generating text 126

Revising   **126**
Style   **127**
The point of punctuation   **128**
Clear words and readability   **129**
Summary   **132**

CHAPTER 08

ARE YOU CONNECTED?   135
Faster and further   135
The internet   136
Email   138
Internet forums   141
Blogs   142
Podcasting   143
Wikis   144
Social networking sites   145
Virtual worlds   147
VoIP   148
Video conferencing   148
Viral marketing   149
Web conferencing (including webinars and webcasts)   149
Instant messaging   150
Mobile phones and texting   151
Blue-jacking and Blue-casting   152

Online advertising	**153**
What's next – Web 2.0?	**154**
Summary	**155**

CHAPTER 09

DOES YOUR TEAM TALK?	157
Crowds, groups and teams	157
The crowd	158
Groups	159
Team or group?	161
What do teams do?	162
First steps	164
How many?	165
Who – and why?	165
Effective team communication	168
Team building	169
Good teams, bad teams	172
Summary	174

CHAPTER 10

WHAT'S YOUR STYLE	177
'Style' – what is it?	177
I'll do it my way	179

I'm OK – you're OK	184
Role theory	188
Assertiveness	190
At the end	194
Summary	194
INDEX	**197**

Preface

Cats do it – subtly, dogs do it – noisily, birds do it – tunefully, whales do it – over long distances and, of course, people do it – in all sorts of places and in all sorts of ways. So, what is it that they all do?

They communicate.

You'll already know how important it is to be able to do this. After all, communication is one of those things that's inextricably interwoven in the 'warp and weft' of all our lives and you've been doing it – or trying to – ever since you were born. But doing it well, getting your communications 'on target' every time, is another thing. Succeeding and getting it right – every time – is important. Do it and you'll enhance the quality and outcomes of your connections with others. Get it wrong – and confusion, frustration, misunderstanding, friction and even anger will follow. There are few places on the planet where getting your communications right is as important as it is in the workplace. Good communication here is so important that it's often described as being 'the fuel that drives its engine'. Making your individual contribution to that 'engine' – and becoming an effective and successful workplace communicator – is just as important. For it's there that you spend your working days and it's there that you go to achieve your hopes and ambitions. So, getting your communication right is significant – after all, it might lead to bigger and better things.

The aim of this book is to help you do just that – get your workplace communication right – and do it well.

Written for people like yourself who manage in a workplace, it's a book that explains and illustrates the what, why, where, when and how of successful workplace communication. It does that in a way that's accessible and easily understood. Rich in diagrams, useful ideas and pointers to appropriate methods and tools, it's *the* book for all of you who wish to develop and learn more about the skills that lead to successful workplace communication. By the time you get to the end of this book you'll not only understand more about what communication is about – you'll also know what you need to do to successfully plan and undertake that workplace communication. By then, if not before, you will have begun, with confidence, the process of becoming a successful workplace communicator.

To get to that point you'll have made your way through the ten chapters of the book. These will tell you about the basic structure of all your communications (Chapter 1), how to listen (Chapter 2), body language (Chapter 3), persuasion and influence (Chapter 4), negotiating (Chapter 5), explaining and presenting (Chapter 6), using both the written word (Chapter 7) and electronic ways of communicating (Chapter 8), groups, teams and communication (Chapter 9) and finding the right style for your communications (Chapter 10). You'll find that each of these chapters:

- starts by telling you what it aims to do and how it will do it
- contains accessible and understandable material that is easily related to your own experience
- finishes with:
  - a summary of the chapter's key points
  - a 'quick tip' that you can take on board instantly to improve your working life.

Above all, it's a book that's aimed at fast-tracking you to where you are an effective and successful workplace communicator.

So what are you waiting for?

Phil Baguley

Acknowledgements

People are always important in the process that leads to the publication of a book like this. In this case, thanks are due to Hodder's Alison Frecknall – who put up with the emails – and Harry Scoble – who found the cover picture, Jill Birch – who's probably the best text editor in the known Universe, Renata Gussone – for her read-through and thoughtful feedback and Linda Baguley, my partner, for the help, counsel, support, edits and read-throughs – as well as the title to Chapter 8.

01

What's it all about?

This chapter starts by looking at the importance of communication in the workplace and then, using a simple model, goes on to take a look at the core elements that come together to make up the communication process. By the end of the chapter, you'll have a clear idea of not only how that process works but also why you use it and some of the factors that can enhance or limit its effectiveness.

Communication – why and when

Let's start with a basic but often overlooked fact about communication. That is that you cannot *not* communicate. When you stand still – you send a message. When you remain silent – you're telling somebody something. When you look away – you're expressing something and when you talk, wave your hands, smile and nod – you're certainly communicating. Whatever you do and however you do it – you're communicating something to somebody.

As a result, there can be little doubt that possessing even modest skill in this process of communication is significant, if not vital, for you. Without that skill, you'll fail to achieve even the most limited of your goals. But, despite its importance, few of us are actually trained in the skills required for *effective* communication. What you do learn, in your home and school, are the basics of how to speak, write and read. Later, at college or university, you used these skills to acquire the specialised knowledge that you needed to do your job and to become, for example, an accountant, a social worker or an engineer. Of course, being able to write, read and speak clearly is important; indeed without these skills you wouldn't be able to get to 'first base' in the communication process. But having these basic skills doesn't necessarily mean that you can communicate well and do it effectively.

Communication in the workplace

The demand for effective communication in the workplace is not only overwhelming, it's also universal. Teachers, doctors, social workers, nurses, salespersons and managers – these are just a few of the workplace roles that demand effective communication if they're going to achieve anything. But, despite the universality of this demand, there are also some workplace roles in which skilled and effective communication is *the* primary core skill that's required.

Being a manager is one of these.

For communicating is something that all managers, whatever their job titles or roles might be, are involved in, all of the time. Studies tell us that they can spend as much as 90 per cent of their time talking to others and almost a third of their time in one-to-one meetings. So being able to communicate effectively will make a considerable difference to your performance as a manager. Yet the picture that you see of communications in most organisations is not a happy one. The majority of managers give little attention to their communication skills and needs and consistently underestimate the amount of time that they spend doing it. Surveys repeatedly tell us that what passes for 'communication' in many organisations is nothing more than people talking *at*, rather than with, each other. As a result, for example, when it comes to decision-making, it's often the person who has spoken the loudest, longest, or with the most conviction that 'wins' – irrespective of whether his or her idea was the best.

Yet communication pervades all that you do as a manager and getting your workplace communication 'right' and moving up to gain success as a workplace communicator can make a significant contribution to your performance. Even small improvements in that process – such as changing your writing style or upgrading your presentation skills – can benefit your working life. Get your communication 'right' and you'll find that it'll lead to:

- increased personal productivity
- higher levels of personal creativity
- improved job satisfaction for you.

As a result, you'll not only do what you need to do better, you'll also enjoy doing it.

So, let's start the journey towards you becoming an effective workplace communicator by taking a look at exactly what is meant by 'communication'.

What is communication?

When it comes to definitions, a dictionary is usually a good place to start. You'll find, for example, that the Oxford English Dictionary tells you that communication involves *'the imparting, conveying, or exchange of ideas, knowledge, information, etc. (whether by speech, writing, or signs)'*. When you check in the typical thesaurus you'll find suggestions that *'interaction'* and *'conversation'* are also relevant. Probe further and you'll find the synonyms – words with the same sense as *'communication'* – of *'intercourse'*, *'transmission'*, *'contact'*, *'connection'* and *'touch'*. As you'd expect, textbooks on communication are more formal. Here, you'll be told that communication is a process *'by which information is passed between individuals and/or organisations by means of previously agreed symbols'*.

But when you think about your own experience of communication you'll soon realise that communication is about more than just passing information. You'll see that it can be about all sorts of things – such as giving praise, expressing displeasure, passing opinions, maintaining or even starting friendships or just simply passing the time of day. Probe a bit further into this pot-pourri and you'll find that when you communicate what's involved are:

- facts
- feelings
- opinions, and
- values.

When you communicate, all of these are conveyed, directly or indirectly, from you to another person or a group of people. This happens (or should happen) when you make a presentation or a speech to a group, crowd or audience or when you talk to, telephone or write to someone else.

This process is extraordinarily versatile. It gets used in a wide range of circumstances and for an even wider variety of purposes. As a result, the definition (for communication) that will be used in this book will be:

COMMUNICATION
Communication is the process that occurs when ideas, information and feelings are conveyed between individuals or groups of individuals for deliberate purposes.

But communication isn't a 'one-purpose-at-a-time' process. When you talk to someone you often convey your feelings as well as ideas or information. When you speak, the content of the message that you send isn't limited to the words spoken. The tone of your voice is a vital part of the message that you send. If you can see the person that you're talking to then gesture, use of space, body contact and facial expression will also add to your message. When you do all of this you communicate information, ideas and feelings simultaneously. One way of looking at the different parts of the message is shown in Figure 1.1.

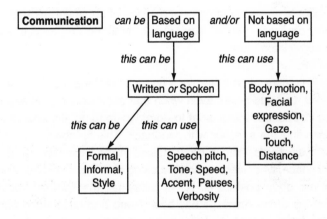

Figure 1.1: Ways of communicating

When you look at this diagram you'll see that your communications can be divided up into those that are, or aren't, based on language. These different ways of communicating are very different. For example, language-based communication draws on the words you use, their meanings and the ways in which you say or write those words. You'll look at the ways that you use words and language in more detail in several of the later chapters of this book. When you don't use words in your communication you use what's often called 'Body Language' – a way of communicating that uses the ways in which you move your body to send your messages. When you think about it you'll soon find that you use this sort of communication a lot – with the smiles, frowns, nods, winks, pointing fingers and hand waves that you use to signal to other people. You'll look at this language in more detail in Chapter 3.

One-way or two-way?

Many people make the mistake of thinking of communication as a one-way process – you tell someone to do something or give him or her some information.

But this isn't so.

For communication is always a two-way process, however and whenever it's undertaken. Even when that communication is about issuing instructions about what to do or where to go, the listener is still providing the speaker with feedback. This feedback doesn't have to use words – it can be contained in the expression on the listener's face, whether he or she is looking at the speaker and what his or her body posture is. All of these tell the speaker about whether his or her message has been heard and understood and what the listener feels about that message or the speaker.

This idea of feedback is important – it changes communication from an inert one-way process to one that's dynamic and two-way. When you think about this you'll soon realise that this feedback can take place at the same time as the message is sent – as, for example, when someone smiles at you when, rather than after, you speak to them. This means that communication can flow in both directions at the same time and can be illustrated as in Figure 1.2.

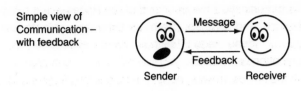

Simple view of
Communication –
with feedback

Figure 1.2: Simple view of Communication – with feedback

If the feedback given is limited – to say, a grunt or a nod – then this sort of communication is often called 'Partial Communication' because the Sender is still the chief communicator. The Receiver, in this instance, is only indicating that he or she has received the communication sent. But it is, nevertheless, an example of two-way communication. The difference between this and 'Full Communication' lies in the fact that feedback in the Partial version does not use words. Nevertheless, as you'll see in Chapter 3, this wordless feedback can be just as meaningful and valid as the original message and in many face-to-face situations this level of feedback is acceptable.

But this can and does change when the feedback is more than just an acknowledgement of the message. When the feedback contains as much information (from the Receiver) as the original message then the process is called Full Communication and the picture changes to that shown in Figure 1.3.

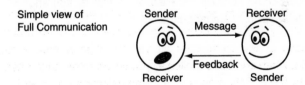

Simple view of
Full Communication

Figure 1.3: Simple view of Full Communication

In Full Communication the Sender and the Receiver are roles that can alternate and overlap. Both of them are able to convey information, ideas and feelings, and examples of Full Communication will include:

- conversations with high levels of openness and intimacy – as between close friends or lovers
- conversations between people with shared concerns or objectives – such as work colleagues or team members.

Full Communication not only gives the Sender feedback about his or her own message – it also gives a message back in return.

Communication channels and noise

But, of course, the Full Communication process isn't quite as simple as that. For example, not all of your thoughts are expressed in speech or writing and when they are you often take care to use words and language that are appropriate – to the subject, the circumstances and the listener or reader. When you do this you use a process called 'encoding' (see Figure 1.4); an example of which would be when you write something and avoid the use of technical jargon that could confuse the Receiver – that is, you encode your message in appropriate language.

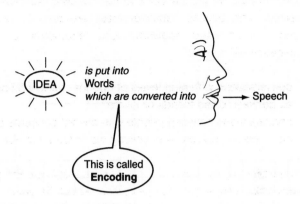

Figure 1.4: Encoding

The reverse process – decoding – happens when the Receiver hears the speech of the message or reads the text. He or she will convert that speech or text from words into an idea or thought – and this is called 'decoding'. Both of these are illustrated in more detail in Figure 1.5 in which Person A:

- thinks of an idea (Idea 1)
- encodes it (Ex)
- transmits it to Person B (Tx).

Person B then receives that idea (Rx), decodes it (Dx) to create Idea 2 and uses it to create another idea (Idea 3) which Person B then encodes and transmits to Person A – who receives and decodes it and uses it to create Idea 4.

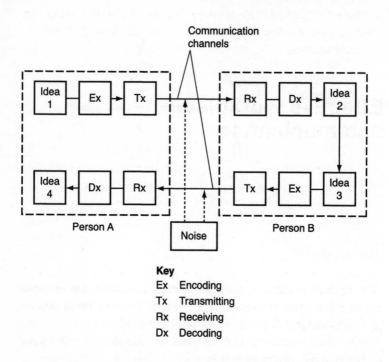

Figure 1.5: The communication process

This figure also introduces two new ideas: a communication channel and communication noise. The first of these – a communication channel – is the medium or mode that you choose to convey your message from you to the other person, such as using the spoken word in a presentation or the written word in a letter. The second of these – communication noise – consists of the external factors that cause a message to become distorted, changed or diminished during transmission – such as distractions, noise, distance or the 'Chinese whispers' or 'Telephone tag' phenomenon – the longer the message chain, the more distorted the message. If you doubt the existence of the Idea 1 → Idea 2 → Idea

3 → Idea 4 sequence that's shown in Figure 1.5 just think about the different ways in which a single word – such as 'love' or 'family' – can be interpreted.

Effective workplace communication

So, now that you've got an idea of the basic structure of all your communications, how are you going to begin to use this to upgrade the effectiveness of your workplace communication?

The first part of the answer to this question comes when you recognise that the shift up to becoming an effective communicator isn't one that happens overnight. It takes patience, time and effort for you to move up from being an ordinary 'hit or miss' communicator to become an effective workplace communicator who hits his or her 'target' every time. But it's not, as you will see in later pages of this book, an impossible task.

The second part of the answer arrives when you meet, understand and use the three 'golden' rules of effective workplace communication. These rules aren't optional; using them and doing that systematically and thoroughly is a 'must-do' if you're going to have any hope of becoming a successful workplace communicator.

The three golden rules

These three golden rules of effective workplace communication are simple and straightforward and based on sound practice that has been proven in a very wide range of workplaces. They tell you that, to be an effective workplace communicator, you must be clear about:

1. **WHO** you are communicating with
2. **WHAT** you're trying to achieve by your communication, and
3. **HOW** you are going to undertake your communication.

So let's look at each of these in turn.

Who are you communicating with?

As a manager, you'll be trying to communicate with a very wide range of people during your working day. If you doubt this, make a list of the people that you talk or write to in an 'average' day – you'll be surprised how long it is! If you're going to communicate effectively with all of these people then you need to be aware of how important it is, when preparing your message, to take into account all that you know about the person you're communicating with. Doing this means that you'll take into account that person's language, language skills and vocabulary, whether he or she is physically near or distant, whether he or she is accessible, whether he or she can see or hear you. Last, but not least, you'll also take into account the message's content.

What do you communicate?

Earlier in this chapter you saw that communication is a process that occurs when ideas, information and feelings are conveyed. All of this takes place because you want to achieve something. That is, your communications are undertaken with aims, objectives, purposes, intentions or outcomes in mind.

But what are these aims, objectives, purposes or outcomes?

When you take time out to think about this question you'll soon find a basic and common answer – that you communicate with other people because you want to influence them or change their behaviour. That is, you want to affect the way that they:

● think and feel about things, and/or
● do things.

If you're going to be successful in your workplace communication then you'll need to make sure that you fully understand and are, at all times, conscious of this basic fact.

But that's not all – take your thinking a little further and you'll soon realise that these aims and objectives will come under one or more of the following headings:

Instructing

When you instruct someone your aim is to change the way in which they act or behave. Simple examples are:

● *The nut A is now placed on the top of screw D.*
● *Write to me when you return.*

Influencing

When you, as a manager, try to influence people the target outcome is a clear and identifiable change in their behaviour. You can do this by motivating, persuading or encouraging them. Influencing is less explicit than instructing and a simple example is: '*If we attain our monthly sales target, it would mean that you all share, under the new incentive scheme, in the benefits of this achievement.*'

Exchanging information

Exchanging information is a two-way process – you give and you also receive information. Both of these need to be taken into account when you plan and conduct your communication.

Giving information

When you give information to someone else you usually do that because they need it to, for example, make a decision or to inform someone else – a customer or a co-worker. The information that you give can be:

- facts – *Turnover was up by 10 per cent last month*
- ideas – *Why don't we do it this way?*
- interpretations based on facts – *She persists in not reacting to falling sales.*
- feelings about all of the above – *I believe that, based on the evidence available, it is time for us to move into a new marketing strategy.*

Seeking information

This is the opposite of Giving information above and can be achieved by:

- asking questions – *How do you do that?'*
- giving information about needs – *I'd like to know more about that*

- showing openness to receiving information – *Yes, I would like to hear about your holiday.*

You can, of course, combine all of these different aims and objectives together in one communication. However, when you do that, you will have to decide what the main and over-riding purpose or objective of that communication is – and do that before you communicate. If you're going to be a successful workplace communicator then there's no room for messages that are confused or confusing or not connected to clear objectives.

How do you communicate?

As an experienced communicator you'll already know that there are some messages that are better written than spoken and some that are better spoken than written. But as an effective and successful workplace communicator you'll need to choose, with care, the way that you send your message. Your message could, for example, be verbal or written, be spoken over a telephone, be part of a face-to-face meeting or be contained in a letter. The communication channel that you choose must be one that gives you a reasonable expectation that the message will be received – and understood.

In general, the factors that you need to be aware of in making that choice are as follows:

The spoken word

- is the most direct form of communication
- can be done formally (interviews) or informally (discussions)
- can be done briefly or at length

- can be recorded but requires additional equipment to do so
- can be an expression of personal style
- can be done with individuals or groups
- can be face-to-face or remote (telephone)
- can make people feel that they have been personally consulted
- can lead to expression of feelings as well as ideas
- enables sharing and comparing
- facilitates non-verbal communication and immediate feedback when face to face
- how it is heard can be influenced by tone and pitch of voice and use of silence.

The written word

- is indirect in nature
- can be formal (a typed letter) or informal (an email, mobile phone text or a handwritten note)
- can be brief or lengthy
- can, for the experienced writer, reflect an individual style
- is often, in organisations, subject to 'rules' about style and presentation
- enables more thought to be put into the choice of words while being written or rewritten
- can be reshaped until the writer is satisfied
- enables the writer to express his or her own ideas and feelings without having to respond to others' reactions and responses
- can be easily copied and so provide physical evidence of transmission and content

- can be sent to a number of people at the same time
- sending copies of documents can be less expensive than having a meeting.

Body language

- requires visual contact between you and the person you're communicating with
- often operates in parallel with the spoken word
- can reinforce, contradict or neutralise the spoken words
- is often more effective at communicating feelings
- is often not consciously used or perceived
- can make a significant difference to effectiveness of communication
- may lead to guesses – not just about what others are thinking or feeling but, more basically, about what kind of person the other is.

Choosing the right mode or medium for your message is a key step towards making sure that your message will be received – and understood. But it's not all that you need to do – for you must also do something about the factors that can and often do cause your communication to fail.

Communication difficulties

You already know that even the best of communications aren't always successful. Earlier in this chapter you saw that communication noise could be one of the causes of this failure to communicate. But that isn't the only cause and other examples of the causes of failure would include illegible or wrongly addressed letters, whispered comments that are misheard and misunderstood, shouted expressions of affection and messages with a warm content that are said without a smile. No doubt you'll be able to add to this list from your own experiences.

So why and how do all of these things happen?

Most of the causes of communication failure are, as you'll soon see, obvious and straightforward. But that doesn't stop them happening and what is needed, if you're going to avoid failure, is the foresight to anticipate these difficulties – and to eliminate them or limit their influence. The following list will give you a fair idea of the major causes of mis-communication – but it isn't exhaustive and you'll probably be able to add some of your own.

- **Lack of clear objectives** leads to uncertainty in the message sent. Most of the time it happens because the person who's sending the message can't decide what to say. This may come about, for example, because they may not know what or how the receiver needs to be told or not wish to offend, upset or shock them.

- **Faulty transmission** means that while the person who's sending the message knows what she or he wants to say, the message is sent by the wrong medium or mode. An example might be sending a personal message in writing when a telephone call or a visit would have been more appropriate, tactful or understanding. Other examples might include speaking too quietly or too slowly – and irritating the listener – or using jargon or inappropriate language. The sender may also expect the receiver to absorb too much information in the time available or may not take into account their prior knowledge (or lack of it!) of the subject of the message.

- **Perception and attitude problems** include those related to false or unstated assumptions or misunderstood messages where the person sending the message might use a word in one context or with one meaning while the person receiving the message would normally use the same word in a different context or with a different meaning. Examples, albeit simple ones, of this would include words such as 'now', 'urgent' and 'quickly'. These problems can also occur when message sender and receiver have viewpoints which are so radically different that the shared understanding that might be generated by talking is not possible. The inability or unwillingness of the person who receives the message to understand or absorb the message is also part of this group as is the behaviour of the person sending the message in withholding information – from fear of the consequences of sharing it or secrecy, deception and lack of trust.

Anticipating and eliminating all of these is a key step towards becoming an effective and successful workplace communicator

Summary

Effective and successful workplace communication is a rare commodity for most managers. However, it is not an optional extra and should be an integral part of all that you do in the workplace. Nevertheless, effective workplace communication can be learnt.

In its basic form communication:

- is a social skill with a purpose
- is a two-way dynamic process
- uses both words and body language.

Communication based on body language uses gesture, posture, space, touch, gaze and expression while communication based on words is about the use of written and spoken language. Effective communication requires thought and planning and involves the choice of the 'right' communication channel. It also requires you to be clear about the objectives of your communications, which can affect other people's thoughts or actions by:

- influencing and/or
- instructing and/or
- exchanging information.

To be successful in your workplace communication you need to be clear about:

1. **WHO** you are communicating with
2. **WHAT** you're trying to achieve by your communication, and
3. **HOW** you are going to undertake your communication.

You also need to anticipate the difficulties that will limit the effectiveness of your communication – and act in ways that eliminate them or limit their influence.

INSTANT TIP

Keep your communication simple. The more complex your means of communication become, the less you actually communicate.

02

Are you listening?

Listening is a skill that's often underrated and, even more often, underused. But listening, and doing it well, is vital to successful communication in the workplace. This chapter starts with a look at how you hear and how that differs from how you do, or don't, listen. It goes on to look, in more detail, at how the act of hearing can be developed into the skill of listening – a skill which is supported by the supplementary skills of attending to and following what others say and reflecting their messages back to them.

Can you hear me?

Hearing is the process by which your body converts variations in the pressure of the air around you into sounds. To do this you use your ears. These have three parts:

1. **Outer ear** This is the flap of skin on the side of your head that people can see. Its main job is to collect sounds but it also includes the ear canal. This canal channels the sound waves in the air around you down towards the next part of your ear.

2. **Middle ear** The main job of this part of the ear is to take those sound waves and turn them into vibrations that are delivered to the inner ear. It uses the eardrum – a thin piece of skin stretched tight like a drum – to do this. The eardrum also separates the outer ear from the middle ear and three tiny bones. All of these vibrate when you hear a sound.

3. **Inner ear** The vibrations in the middle ear enter the cochlea – a small, curled tube in the inner ear. This is filled with liquid, which is set in motion by these vibrations. It's also lined with tiny hairs that move when the liquid moves. It's these hair sensors that convert air movement into nerve signals that are sent to your brain and that your brain understands as sound. However, these hairs are also made up of one of the few body cells that do not regenerate when damaged. As a result they can become irreparably damaged by loud noise.

All of this is shown in Figure 2.1.

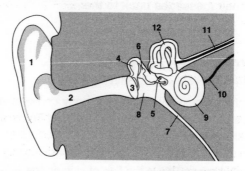

1 Pinna	7 Eustachian tube
2 Auditory canal	8 Tympanuem cavity
3 Tympaniac membrane	9 Cochlea
(ear drum)	10 Auditory nerve
4 Malleus	11 Vesticular nerve
5 Stapes	12 Semi-circular canals
6 Incus	

Figure 2.1: The ear

Your ears can hear quite a wide range of sounds, typically from 15Hz to 20,000Hz in frequency. But this will change as you get older – more than 50 per cent of people over the age of 60 have a hearing loss – or if you overexpose yourself to loud noises. As this age-related hearing loss begins to show itself when you reach the age of 40, it's quite possible that you'll be communicating with people in your workplace who suffer from it. If you're going to communicate effectively with these people you'll need to take this hearing loss into account – by, for example, speaking slowly and clearly and looking directly at the person when you're speaking. When it comes to what's heard, some animals are much better at it than we are. Bats and dogs, for example, can hear sounds at higher frequencies (ultrasonic sounds) than us and elephants, whales and giraffes can hear sounds at lower frequencies (infrasonic sounds) than we are able to hear.

But your ears can do a lot more than just hear. They also keep you balanced and, because you have two of them, they enable you to locate the direction or source of a sound. A sound from your left, for example, will reach your left ear before it reaches your right ear or will be slightly louder in your left ear than it is in your right ear. When your brain detects these differences it (and you) conclude that the sound is coming from your left.

Listening and hearing

Now that you know what hearing is and how it happens, it's time to take a look at the process that is called listening. Listening and hearing are different. When you dig into your dictionary what you'll find are definitions like these:

Hearing: *To perceive, or have the sensation of, sound; to possess or exercise the faculty of audition, of which the specific organ is the ear.*

> Listening: *To hear attentively; to give ear to; to pay attention to (a person speaking or what is said).*

When you read around the subject of listening you'll also find it described as a process that needs 'active participation' and is the outcome of 'deliberate, active behaviour'. These and other definitions tell you that:

● hearing is a passive, reflexive, almost automatic response,

While

● listening is a chosen, deliberate action.

Research backs this up, concluding that while almost all of us can hear, few of us can and do listen properly. The average person, for example, is said to remember about a half of what they hear immediately afterwards and, in some tests, an alarmingly low 10 per cent of what's heard after three hours! This tells you that skill in listening is not a natural ability – it's one that has to be learnt. What usually happens when someone is talking is that you don't listen because you are:

● preoccupied with something or someone else
● waiting to find a gap so that you can speak
● preparing what you want to say in response to what the speaker is saying
● reviewing your own personal beliefs about what is being said
● making judgements about the speaker or the message
● finding excuses to avoid asking for clarification when you know that you don't understand what's being said.

None of these help you to listen and this situation is often made worse by the fact that you'll hide your non-listening by pretending to listen. Table 2.1 gives further illustrations of the ways in which we do that. Check them out and see if you recognise any.

Table 2.1: Ways of pretending to listen

Pretend listening You pretend to listen but are actually listening to another conversation in the room, or thinking about something else.

Point-scoring listening You relate everything you hear to your own experience: *'Oh! that's nothing. Wait till you hear what happened to me last week!'*

Predictive listening You predict what the other person is really thinking and say to yourself, *'I bet that's not the real reason she came here.'*

Rehearsal listening You practise what you are going to say next and miss what is being said.

Selective listening You listen for a key piece of information and then stop listening.

Filling the gaps listening You throw in a word when there is a natural pause.

Labelling listening You put the person talking into a category and then filter what's said: *'A typical salesman!'*

Duelling listening You intervene here and there with a defensive remark: *'Well, at least we don't do that.'*

Side-stepping listening You respond to expressions of emotion with clichés or jocular remarks: *'It's not the end of the world is it?'*

This unsatisfactory situation is further complicated by the fact that, when somebody is speaking, you 'filter' what you hear. We all have these hearing filters and they reflect a very wide range of factors – such as how you're feeling, what your beliefs are, what you do or don't value, the sort of culture you've grown up in, what you're expecting to be said, your attitude towards the speaker or the organisation he or she represents, your personality, attitude, interests and past experiences. All of these, and more, influence what you allow yourself to listen to or even hear. This 'filtering' happens quite unconsciously, leaving you unaware of how much it colours and limits what you allow yourself to listen to. Becoming aware of these 'filters' and choosing not to use them is an important step on your path to becoming a better listener.

Why listen?

The benefits of changing this sort of situation are considerable. There are many, many workplace situations in which your ability to listen – rather than just hear – can make a major contribution to your performance. For example, being able to listen in formal negotiations not only to what is said but also the way that it is said can provide you with valuable information – information that might enable you to overcome an impasse or exploit an advantage. In day-to-day situations your ability to listen is just as important. For, by really listening, not only will you gain access to valuable facts, opinions and information – you'll also gain the respect and co-operation of your co-workers. When you are interviewing, your ability to question *and* listen skilfully is a key issue for both you and the person you are interviewing. From these and other examples in your own experience you'll soon see that listening effectively can make a big difference to your job performance.

For being able to listen carefully and effectively will get you to where you:

- **possess more information** – and, as a consequence, make better decisions and are better able to understand what is expected of you in the assignments and projects that you're given
- **have better relationships** – and, as a consequence, are able to build a better rapport with co-workers, bosses, and clients
- **better understand co-workers** – and, as a consequence, are more effective in a team-based environment (see Chapter 9)
- **are better at resolving problems** – because you are better able to understand the other's point of view
- **are less defensive and more encouraging** – because you become more aware of the underlying meanings in what others say.

So how can you get to the place where you can do all of this or, to put it another way, how can you step up from just hearing to become an effective listener?

First steps to effective listening

The process of becoming an effective listener begins, as you've already seen, with the act of hearing. Being able to hear, accurately and clearly, what is being said to you is an important but obvious first step towards effective listening. In fact, it's so important that it's worth some further thought and comment. So, if you have been finding (as most of us do when we get older) it harder to understand what's being said in conversation, especially when there's background noise, or if sounds sometimes seem muffled, or if you're having to turn the volume up when you listen to the television – then visit your doctor or an audiologist and get your hearing checked out.

But even if your hearing is OK there are still some basic steps that you can take towards 'good' hearing:

- **Position yourself to hear** – face the person that you're talking to.
- **Turn off or reduce background noise and distractions** – switch off your mobile phone, close the office door.
- **Choose quiet settings** – choose a place to talk that's away from noisy areas.

Doing all of these will help you to hear better. But that isn't enough. For effective listening isn't just about hearing the words that people say. As you saw in Chapter 1, a lot of what you communicate is delivered non-verbally or by the spaces and pauses around the words that are spoken. Studies of spoken and line-of-sight workplace communication tell us that:

- the words spoken provide less than one-tenth of the message
- the way those words are spoken provides around four-tenths of the message, and
- body language – such as facial expressions, posture, gestures, eye contact – provide the remaining half of the message.

When you think about these figures you'll soon realise that, while hearing what is said contributes a small proportion of the total message, listening to the way it's said contributes a much larger part of the message. If you can see the person talking, things like the way that they look at you, their facial and body movements and posture all make a significant contribution to the total message.

You'll look at these and other aspects of 'body language' in more detail in Chapter 3 but, for now, it's worth noting how important they are.

Even if you can't see the person that you're talking to there's a lot more information coming your way than just mere words. This extra information will include:

- the emphasis that's placed on the words spoken
- the number and frequency of the pauses between the words or sentences spoken
- the pitch, stress and volume of these spoken words or sentences.

Additionally, the speaker's tone of voice can often convey more meaning than his or her words. Pauses, for example, can make up as much as 40 per cent of speech and can tell you that the speaker is being thoughtful or planning what to say next. But when pauses are used in excess, they can suggest that the person who's talking lacks self-confidence or is anxious or uncertain. The way that spoken words are, or aren't, stressed also adds meaning to a sentence and focuses your attention on particular words. The pitch of the spoken word is also used to indicate the emotion behind the words – with anger being shown by a sudden increase in pitch, surprise by a rising pitch, contempt by a fall in pitch at the end of a sentence and questioning by a rise in pitch at the end of a sentence.

When you think about all of these factors you'll soon realise that if you're going to listen effectively you're going to have to take into account a lot more than just what is said. Let's take a look at how you can do that.

How to listen effectively

To listen effectively you need to acquire and use a unique package of skills. These skills are usually described as those associated with:
- attending
- following, and
- reflecting.

Let's look at each of these in turn.

Attending

The skills that you use when you attend are often described as the 'body language' skills of listening. They are the 'building blocks' of good listening and include:

- **Posture** – adopting a posture of relaxed alertness indicates that you're accepting and paying attention to what the speaker says. It often helps to:
  - sit forward and incline your body toward the speaker
  - face the speaker squarely and head on
  - keep an open position with your arms and legs unfolded.
- **Movement** – try to avoid motions and gestures that distract and keep your movements responsive to the speaker's movements.
- **Eye contact** – when used well this tells the speaker that you're interested in what she or he is saying. When used to excess, it can be scary as well as implying levels of intimacy that may not be appropriate.

Following

These are the skills that are aimed at encouraging the speaker to speak. To be effective they've got to act in ways that don't get in the way of he or she doing so. This means that when you use them you shouldn't ask too many questions, or ask questions that divert the conversation in directions the speaker doesn't want to go.

Following skills also include:

- **Using 'Door Openers'** – these, as opposed to 'door slammers', are open-ended responses that don't convey evaluation or judgement. Examples include questions and comments such as 'What's on your mind?', 'What do you think?' or 'Would you like to tell me more about that?' and 'That's a good question'. They should only be used when you really do have time available for the conversation. Using a 'door opener' and then cutting the response short isn't an intelligent use of your listening skills.
- **Using Encouragers** – when used in good listening these say very little, but do encourage the speaker to continue talking. They do this because they tell the speaker that you are interested and you're following what they are saying. Encouragers like this include nodding your head or saying 'mm-hmm' or 'go on'.
- **Asking Questions** – if your questions are going to work then they have to be infrequent, limited in number and aimed at drawing the speaker out.
- **Being Silent** – most people find silence difficult. But allowing silence in a conversation does give the speaker space to think, feel and find the way to express him or herself. You can use the silent pauses in a conversation to observe facial expressions, posture and gestures or to think about what the other person is communicating. Being silent can also, in the right circumstances, be an effective way of communicating.

Reflecting

This is, without doubt, the most difficult of all the skills of listening. It involves restating, in a way that demonstrates understanding and acceptance, the content of and feelings behind what the speaker has said. However, there will be situations in which, as a manager, you may feel that the use of reflective techniques is not appropriate – you may feel that you need to argue, advise or confront. On these occasions you'll need to switch from being reflective to be directive. However, you can and should use reflective techniques when you:

● need or want to understand the other person's feelings more fully, or
● sense that the other person has not yet revealed or is not sure about his or her thoughts and feelings about the situation.

Here you can use reflective responses initially – until you feel that you really understand the person's perspective – and then switch to a more directive or confrontational or persuasive stance.

Reflecting skills involve:

● **Paraphrasing**, in your own words and concisely, the core content of the speaker's communication.
● **Reflecting feelings** by mirroring back to the speaker, in a succinct statement, the emotions which he or she is presenting.
● **Reflecting meaning** by, simply, concisely and thoughtfully, reflecting both the speaker's content and emotion.
● **Summarising** by restating the overall themes and feelings of what's been said.

Acquiring all of these skills of effective listening isn't an overnight event. It takes time and practice to hone and polish the how and when of their use. But making this commitment – to effective listening – is worthwhile. For not only is effective listening, at its core, a social skill, it's also one that will take you further down the road of demonstrating that what we can achieve together can be greater than the sum of our individual contributions.

Table 2.2 gives you a set of guidelines that should help to make your listening more effective.

Ways and means

Most of your workplace communication will happen when you talk and listen to people. This will typically take place in informal small groups. As the roots of this sort of thing lie way back in humankind's early history, you'll not be surprised to find that a number of words have evolved to describe what goes on in these groups and meetings. The most commonly used of these are:

- conversations
- discussions
- debates, and
- dialogues.

But, despite the fact that they all describe what goes on when we talk and listen to each other, there are major differences between them – as you'll now see.

Table 2.2: Good guide to listening

1. **Indicate by your manner that what is being said is being absorbed**
   - look, encourage by nodding, and reinforce: *'I see.'*
2. **Avoid self/others interrupting**
   - don't interrupt, unless it is to ask for clarification
   - stop or avoid others interrupting.
3. **Resist distractions**
   - listen for the theme of the message
   - focus on what the speaker is saying
   - avoid verbal, visual or physical distractions.
4. **Don't judge content or delivery**
   - concentrate on listening without judging.
5. **Avoid daydreaming**
   - make yourself listen, don't tune out
   - maintain eye contact, lean forward, occasionally summarise: *'So you are saying…'*
6. **Let him or her talk**
   - don't rush to fill the speaker's pauses
   - if the speaker stops, encourage him or her to continue: *'Go on'* or *'What happened then?'*
7. **Keep your mind open**
   - listen in an understanding way
   - don't prejudge what they will say before they've said it.
8. **Listen between the words**
   - be alert for omissions: sometimes the essential message is contained in what is *not* said
   - listen for feeling as well as meaning
   - ask yourself is the speaker:
     - critical or neutral? • optimistic or pessimistic?
     - confident or defensive? • open or evasive?
9. **Check your interpretation of the speaker's message**
   - clarify by: *'So the situation is …?'* or *'Do you mean …?'*
   - ask questions if you don't understand
   - ask yourself: *'Do I really know what they are saying?'*

Conversations

Workplace conversations usually involve no more than three people – more than that and they become discussions. They are usually informal, polite, short in duration and conflict free but can be social – as in those that start (and finish) with the question 'How are you?' – or collaborative – in which participants come together with a shared and agreed purpose. They are the most common form of verbal communication and can be conducted face-to-face or by using a telephone or real time instant messaging.

Discussions

Discussions are different from conversations. They involve an oral exploration of a topic, object, concept or experience. They are also more formal, take longer, involve more people and take place less often than conversations. They are usually face-to-face events but can, by use of technology (see Chapter 8), be conducted by people at a distance from one another. They usually involve the examination or investigation of a subject or issue and, if successful, generate a decision about that subject or issue. These discussions can be about work that's been done, work that needs to be done, avoiding pitfalls, finding shortcuts or making sure that the resources necessary to do the job are available. If these discussions are going to be effective then they need to be interactive in a way that builds rapport and talks about goals, deadlines, guidelines and specifications. They can also take the form of an internet-based discussion forum in which user A posts a question to which user B posts an answer and user C and others view both question and answer. But, even in the best ordered of workplaces, disagreements can occur. When this happens your communication with your co-workers will shift up into debate.

Debate

A debate is, at its core, an argument. But it's usually an argument that's conducted in a formal manner between groups of people and by using procedural rules designed to ensure that both sides of an issue are discussed. The outcome is a decision about which viewpoint is 'right'. In the workplace, these sorts of debate take place in meetings about issues such as which project will be funded or which make or type of computer will be bought. The outcome of such a debate is decided by voting. Informal workplace debates are also common, but the quality of their outcomes is very dependent upon the knowledge and skill of people involved. They can be constructive and rational with issues and principles argued logically and outcomes generated or they can shift into the sort of disordered and chaotic debate in which conflicts surface but are rarely resolved. Outside the workplace, debates are common events in the UK Parliament or the Scottish and Welsh Assemblies.

Dialogue

A workplace dialogue is an unusual and rare event. It has been described as a conversation where there is a 'free flow of meaning in a group and diverse views and perspectives are encouraged'. Real dialogues involve discarding your biases and allowing the free flow of diverse views and perspectives. Dialogues like this can be very creative and because of this they are worth working towards. But there are three conditions that must be met if your dialogues are going to work. For you must:

1. Suspend assumptions.
2. Regard each other as colleagues.
3. Use a facilitator to hold the context of dialogue.

Good dialogues lead to the sort of creative thinking that emerges when genuine listening, mutual respect, suspended judgement and authentic inquiry work together. It's described as 'an activity of curiosity, co-operation, creativity, discovery, and learning rather than persuasion, competition, fear, and conflict'.

What all of this shows you is that there will be a shift up in both effectiveness and outcomes as you move your workplace communications up through the following sequence:

conversation → discussion → debate → dialogue.

However, you'll always need to listen effectively and Table 2.3 Listening Skills Self-evaluation questionnaire will help to check out your understanding of what it takes to become an effective listener.

Table 2.3: Listening Skills Self-evaluation Questionnaire

Ring the number that's closest to the way you do it. Then add up your total score.

ATTENDING

1. Gaze

We had good eye contact	**1 2 3 4 5 6 7**	We had no eye contact

2. Posture

I adopted an open posture with no crossed arms and legs	**1 2 3 4 5 6 7**	I crossed my arms and legs

3. Position

I faced him/her and leant forward	**1 2 3 4 5 6 7**	I turned away and sat back

4. Distractions

I did something about distractions	**1 2 3 4 5 6 7**	I did nothing about the distractions

Table 2.3: *Continued*

LISTENING

1. Silence

| I allowed silences and did not break them | **1 2 3 4 5 6 7** | I found silences difficult and spoke to break them |

2. Interrupting

| I did not interrupt | **1 2 3 4 5 6 7** | I interrupted persistently |

3. Questions

| I asked clarifying questions | **1 2 3 4 5 6 7** | I asked irrelevant questions |
| I asked open questions | **1 2 3 4 5 6 7** | I asked closed questions |

4. Relaxation

| I felt relaxed but attentive | **1 2 3 4 5 6 7** | I felt tense and ill at ease |

SCORING

If your total score comes to 27 or less then you are listening. Scores of 36 and above indicate that you may be having some problems listening to what is said to you. A score for an individual question of four or above tells you where you need to improve.

Summary

Listening is an underrated and often underused skill that's vital to the art of successful communication. It is a deliberate, active behaviour that starts with the reflex of hearing but goes on beyond that to involve the act of hearing attentively. Increasing the effectiveness of your listening can make a big difference to your job performance.

Listening effectively means taking into account a lot more than the words spoken – you also need to be aware of the way that those words are spoken and the speaker's body language. To do that you need to develop and learn how to use the skills of:

- attending
- following
- reflecting.

Listening in the workplace will take place in conversations, discussions, debates and dialogues. The most powerful and creative of these is the dialogue which, as 'an activity of curiosity, co-operation, creativity, discovery, and learning rather than persuasion, competition, fear, and conflict' can lead to the generation of highly creative solutions.

INSTANT TIP

The first step to effective listening is to stop talking.

03

Why didn't he (or she) smile?

Most of what you communicate to other people is contained in the spaces between and around the words that you use. It's there that you'll find the messages that are given by the ways in which you stand, look (or don't look) at each other, smile, scowl and gesture. These are far more eloquent than words – but are often only used unconsciously. This chapter argues that if you are going to be a successful and effective communicator then you need to be able to understand and be fluent in the use of this 'other language' and suggests how that might be achieved.

Bodily communication

You've already seen – earlier in this book – how important body language is to the ways and means of your communication. In fact, it's so important that it's worth reminding you about what the research studies tell us. For these say that in spoken and line-of-sight workplace communication:

- the words spoken provide less than one-tenth of the message
- the way those words are spoken provides around four-tenths of the message, and
- body language – such as facial expressions, posture, gestures, eye contact – provide the remaining half of the message.

Using your body – instead of words – to communicate with other people is a way of doing things that's been around for a long time. In the earliest days of humankind – before we, as a species, developed language skills – it must have been the only way to tell each other about things such as food, threats, safe havens and even feelings. Nowadays, of course, things are different and you can talk and write to people on the other side of the planet as and when you please.

But are things really that different?

For your bodily (or non-verbal) communications still provide the majority of the content of the line-of-sight messages that you send to other people. But why is this so, why in the twenty-first century are you still using your body to communicate?

The answer to this question is neither simple nor straightforward. For there will always be circumstances and situations in which waving or gesturing is the only effective way to communicate (see Figure 3.1).

There also seems to be some evidence that using your body to communicate is an innate or 'hard wired' potentiality for human beings. You start to turn this potentiality into an actuality at an early age – before you learn to speak – and then continue to practise and refine it throughout the rest of your life. As a child you learnt non-verbal expressions by watching and imitating, and were generally more adept at both reading and using these than the adults around you.

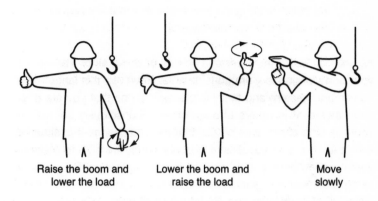

Raise the boom and lower the load   Lower the boom and raise the load   Move slowly

Figure 3.1: Cranesman hand signals

Now, when you use non-verbal communication, a number of things happen – though not all of them come about because of a conscious choice on your part. For non-verbal communication enables you to:

- overcome the limitations that words sometimes have – as, for example, when explaining shapes or indicating directions
- gain an additional and separate communication channel that enables you to expand the complexity or meaning of a verbal message.

But those aren't the only things that happen when you use body language. For when you do that, you also:

- hint at, signal or even express your inner feelings
- give messages that are often seen to be more genuine than your spoken messages

● often express or hint at feelings that are inappropriate to the place or situation that you're in – that are beyond the boundaries of 'social etiquette'.

As you can see, the power and effects of doing all of this – using your body language – are considerable. However, this language of movement, gesture and facial expression is one that you are often more aware of in others (though often unconsciously so) than in yourself. One of the aims of this chapter is to change that situation – so that you, as a successful communicator, are able to enhance your ability to both 'speak' and 'read' body language. But, in order to do that, you are going to have to take a look at some of the 'science' of body language. So let's do that now.

The science of body language

The study of bodily communication is not new. Interest in the how and why of the ways in which bodily movements contribute to communication has been around for a long time – particularly in connection with public speaking and drama. However, it's only in the last 70 or so years that this science has taken a major step forward – reflecting the presence of easily available facilities for recording and analysing human movements. Nowadays, digital technology has enabled these studies to be extended even further.

As a result, the lexicon of words used to describe the aspects of bodily communication has grown and Table 3.1 shows some of the more important ways of describing the ways that you communicate using your body. When you look at these you'll see that the factors that are said to contribute to your bodily communications show a considerable range and diversity.

Table 3.1: Non-verbal communication

Ways and Means

Kinesics – hand, arm, leg, head and eye movements, posture changes, gaze and facial expressions

Proxemics – distance and spacing, territorial factors

Tacesics – body contact and touching

Body appearance – body shape, skin colour, smell

Use of ornamentation – clothes , jewellery, wigs, hair, etc.

There's also just as much diversity displayed when it comes to the uses that you make of these 'modes' of communication. For example, in a face-to-face conversation you can use bodily communication to:

- repeat what's been said – as in saying 'that way' and pointing
- contradict what's been said – as in saying 'I'm happy' without a smile
- substitute for words – as in shaking your head instead of saying 'no'
- complement words – as in saying 'I'm happy' and smiling
- relate to and regulate conversations by nods, eye movements and posture shifts.

What you'll do now is to look in more detail at some of the more common forms of bodily communication.

Gestures

We all use gestures a lot. When you gesture, you send a visual signal to someone. These gestures can be deliberate – as in a wave of recognition, incidental – as in the hand movements associated with a sneeze, or unconscious – as when you scratch your head when thinking about something. Most of your gestures will involve hands but your head and other parts of the body can also take part.

Your conscious gestures can be categorised as follows:

Emblems

Emblems are deliberate gestures that have a direct verbal equivalent. Usually involving hand movements, you'll use them in situations where:

- verbal communication is difficult , or
- speed or privacy or visibility over a distance are needed.

Used in a wide range of work situations – by fire-fighters, crane drivers and TV studio floor managers – they often require the 'observer' to know what they mean. They are also said to cross cultural and language barriers.

Illustrators

Illustrators are also used deliberately and are directly linked to speech. However, their purposes are to illustrate, repeat, complement or underline what has been said. Examples include:

- guide signs – such as pointing or beckoning
- spatial signs – such as movements about 'up' or 'around'
- form or shape gestures – which describe a shape in space
- bodily action signs – which mimic or replicate body actions.

Regulators

Regulator gestures are used in your conversations. They are used, for example, to show your interest in what's being said and to signal that you want to say something.

Unconscious gestures are just as important as their conscious counterparts. They are often called 'leakage' gestures – because they display or hint at your inner and often hidden feelings, thoughts and emotions. They will occur despite your best efforts to control them and despite the pressure of social 'rules' about controlling your gestures or expressing emotions. Simple and commonly seen examples include your actions of:

- touching your body when under stress, in ways that replicate or mimic the actions of others when they are comforting you – such as hugging yourself
- covering your mouth with a hand when wishing to mislead or deceive others.

Facial expressions

We all read faces. It's such a common thing for us to do that we often don't realise that we're doing it. And, of course, other people read our faces. The expressions that you show on your face are rich in information about your thoughts, feelings and intentions. Like your gestures, these facial expressions can be deliberate – as with the polite 'social' smile, or incidental – as when you screw your eyes up in bright sunlight, or unconscious – as when you are genuinely surprised, shocked or alarmed.

In social situations your facial expressions are observed closely by others and can provide considerable information about your emotions and attitudes. However, some of these expressions – such as a smile, laugh or frown – can be very easily faked. Nevertheless, other facial expressions – such as those involving small movements of your lip and jaw muscles and the muscles around your eyes – are much more difficult to fake and do provide clues about genuine, rather than pretended, feelings.

Almost all of your facial expressions are to do with communicating your feelings and emotions. As a very young child you were able to use your facial expressions to show your fear, hunger, anger, surprise and happiness. Since then you've extended your repertoire of facial expressions to the point where you can use them to show a very wide range of emotions. When you do this you employ facial movements of considerable complexity involving co-ordinated movements of muscles in and around the eyes, forehead, eyebrows, brow, cheeks, nose, jaw and lips. Research on these facial expressions has identified over 30 basic elements of facial expression as well as 45 positions for the face, 17 for the eyes, and 8 brow and forehead positions.

Gaze

When you gaze at someone you look at them in a steady or fixed way. This gazing can be done for a short or a long time, by one person or both and can take place while talking or listening. It can also be expressive, direct or indirect and can generate a wide range of responses on the part of the 'gazed-at' person. Animals gaze a lot and do so to send signals as well as collect information.

Our close cousins, the monkeys, will, for example, often use gaze to threaten – as in staring someone down – or to signal alliance and affiliation. Similarly, people use gaze in a wide variety of ways. Lovers gaze into each other's eyes while others, usually men, use extended gaze to express dominance and aggression. Gaze even affects those being gazed at as speakers who gaze a lot are seen by those listening to them to be more credible and persuasive.

In most social situations, however, your gazing will be limited by social rules or norms – such as 'it's not polite to stare'. As a result your social gazing is discontinuous and involves glances of a limited duration. Nevertheless, even small changes in this sort of gazing will often signal things like the desire to start or finish a conversation. This happens because you look at those you wish to communicate with and generally do so before you start to speak. You also, when speaking, will glance at people in order to confirm their attention or to underline or emphasise what is being said. Using gaze to communicate with those around you is a common and well-used pattern of behaviour – despite the fact that the rules of gaze are complex and sometimes misunderstood or misinterpreted.

Touching

Bodily contact or touch is a way of communicating that you first experience when you are a child. Much of the warmth and affection that you received from your parents was expressed as intimate body contact in the form of strokes, caresses, pats, kisses and embraces. As you grow older, your body contact with your parents lessens and becomes limited to kisses, embraces and handshakes and your close, extensive and intimate body contact begins and continues to involve your very close friends and sexual partners.

Nevertheless, body contact or touch does take place with other people who aren't family members or sexual partners. These contacts can be either social – as in a handshake – or non-social – as when the toucher has a role that requires touching, such as a doctor, dentist or hairdresser. Unless you carry out one of those roles, almost all of your workplace touching will be social in nature. As such, it will include such actions as:

- greeting people by shaking hands or embracing
- influencing people by touching their arm, hand or shoulder while speaking
- directing or guiding people by a light clasp on the arm or a slight touch to the back.

There are many variations of these basic forms of social touching. Most of them reflect the nature and intimacy of the relationship between the toucher and the touched. For example, touch initiated by high status individuals in the workplace is more likely to be an expression of dominance than an expression of affection. But touch in the workplace does have its downside as it is often associated with sexual harassment. The level and type of social touching that is acceptable differs between cultures. For example, Arab, South American and Southern European cultures are often seen as 'contact' cultures while Japanese, British and North American cultures are seen as 'non or low-contact' cultures. It's also said that kissing and hugging in the workplace is more common in the 'creative' industries – such as publishing.

Using space

Space tends to be a scarce and expensive commodity in most workplaces. As a result, the ways that you position yourself in that space and the closeness or proximity that you allow yourself to tolerate are not only important to others – they also make a difference to the effectiveness of your communications. For we all have an individual definition of what is called our 'personal space'.

Research tells us that this is typically circular in shape with you being positioned nearer to the front than the rear of the circle. The size of this circle or personal space will reflect your individual:

- psychological and physical needs
- preferences about the distance between yourself and others.

It will also be influenced by your age, gender, status, like or dislike of the other person and the nature of the discussion that you're having with them. Researchers also tell us that how close you get to somebody depends on what you're doing with them. For example, intimate stuff – such as touching, feeling body heat, smelling and whispering – takes place when you are either in contact or no more than half a metre away from each other. Beyond this zone and up to about a metre and half of separation is the personal zone in which most of our two-to-three-people conversations take place. In this zone you can see, easily hear and touch each other but can't smell body odours or perfumes or feel body heat. Beyond this zone and up to about 4 metres of separation is the social zone in which most meetings, presentations and interviews take place. Because of these higher separation distances, speech and gaze are used more often in this zone. Beyond the social zone you enter what's usually called the public zone in which large groups of people are addressed. Because of the separation distances involved, things like emphasised verbal cues, body posture and gestures are needed to replace the eye contact and facial expression used in the inner zones.

Posture

The ways that you stand, sit, recline, lean, place or cross your arms and lower or tilt your head all form a part of what is called your 'posture'. But when you look this word up in the dictionary you'll find things like 'stance', 'body position' and, surprisingly, 'attitude' are cited as definitions of this word. However, this is as it should be – because the postures that you adopt will often reveal much of how you feel about others. For example, if you see that someone is sitting stiffly or rigidly this could indicate that the person is tense or with someone they dislike or fear. A relaxed posture could indicate that the person feels that they are of higher status or rank than those around them or are with someone they like. But the posture that you adopt doesn't just tell others about how you feel, it can also work the other way – to induce an emotion in you. For example, research tells us that when people sit in a slumped, head-down, depressed position they appear to develop feelings of helplessness more readily than when they sit in an expansive, upright posture.

But the postures that you adopt are not only an expression of how you feel, they are also often the postures that are approved for that situation by the 'culture' in which you live or work. There are, for example, 'correct' postures for eating, giving a lecture or presentation, being interviewed, sunbathing and riding a horse. If you don't adopt the 'correct' posture then you may be seen as 'uncivilised' or 'eccentric'. Posture is also used differently by men and women – men, for example, usually sit with knees and ankles apart while women sit with knees and ankles together or only slightly apart. Posture on its own will rarely tell you all that you need to know about what people are thinking or feeling. Nevertheless, it can provide a rich source of information when taken with other signals such as facial expression and gesture.

Appearance

Your personal appearance is made up from a complex mix of many factors. Your height and build, whether you do or don't wear make-up, your hair, hands, overall fitness, whether you have a tattoo or pierced ears and what sort of clothes and jewellery or badges you wear – all of these and many other factors blend together to create your individual appearance. This appearance is important. For studies tell us that people make judgements about you and your character from the way that you appear to them. And they do this very quickly – within the first ten seconds of meeting you!

Your appearance – or the way that you appear to others – can, for example:

- tell them about your chosen 'self-image', or
- tell them whether you're a member of a club or organisation, or
- tell them what your job is.

Clothes play a major role in your appearance. They can, for example, give signals about your personality, social status, attitude towards others, whether you are, or aren't, sexually available and whether you are, or aren't, concerned about what's 'fashionable'.

Most of the time you choose the clothes that you wear in order to either influence what others think of you or conform to what's 'normal' for the situation. For example, you'll wear a suit for a job interview and a dinner jacket or formal dress for a formal dinner.

But your appearance is actually quite flexible. You can, for example, easily change the way that you:

- dress
- do your hair
- tint your skin and hair colour, and
- smell.

You can also change the badges, jewellery and other accessories that you wear and you might even go to the extreme of having plastic surgery to, for example, change the shape of your nose or face and remove some signs of ageing.

When you change your appearance, it's done with a purpose: that of influencing the impressions or perceptions that others have about you. For your appearance can influence and colour these impressions significantly and people will often adjust how they behave towards you based on how they see you.

How to use body language

You've already seen how important your body language is. It provides the majority of the information that you send to those around you and does so in ways that you will often be unaware of. So understanding the how and why of body language is worth the effort. For not only will it improve your day-to-day communications, it'll also contain the potential to improve the quality of your life.

So here are some tips as to how you might do that.

1. Be body conscious

This doesn't mean that you should be body self-conscious. It does mean that you should try to be more aware of the ways that you use your body language. Other people actually, whether you like it or not, do spend a lot of time looking at or 'reading' your body language. So try to identify your own body language patterns – the sorts of things that you habitually do in the different sorts of exchanges that you have with different people. Using a mirror in the privacy of your own home is one good way of starting this – see if you can identify what your body does when you're angry, happy, worried, etc. It is also worth taking a look at your own facial expressions. Being conscious of your body language can also help you to understand how you feel. If you're not quite sure about how you're feeling in a particular situation, pay attention to what your body is saying. When you do this you should, with practice, be able to read your own body language as well as anybody else can and so learn more about yourself and your reactions to workplace situations.

2. Act unaffectedly

When you first start to study body language you'll quickly find that there are books, articles and encyclopedia-like works of reference that'll tell you about every possible posture, gesture and muscle tic that you're likely to meet. Mastering and using all of this information represents a considerable task. But that's not all that it is; for it's also a task that *won't* necessarily add to your ability to communicate using body language. For the reality is that the meanings of these signals differ – not only from person to person but also from culture to culture. So, instead of trying to consciously control every gesture or facial expression, try to relax and, above all, be natural.

3. Be body positive

The easiest way to do this is to make sure that your body language is 'in sync' with your words. When you do this you'll be able to communicate more clearly and will be seen as being more 'charismatic' when you do that. But that isn't all that you'll need to do to make your body language 'positive'. For you can also do a host of other things including:

- stopping persistently touching your face – as this tells people that you're anxious
- sit up and stand with a straight back but open posture – as doing this tells people that you're confident and relaxed

- when you're talking to somebody, direct the most positive gestures toward the listener and the negative gestures away from yourself and the listener
- stay calm – whatever is happening – as when you do that you are more likely to be free and open, rather than withdrawn or defensive.

4. One step at a time

If you're changing some feature of your body language it's best to take it slowly and take it steady. Remember that most of the people with whom you interact in the workplace will know you fairly well. So they'll be used to reading your particular brand of body language, which, incidentally, means that they're less likely to misinterpret your non-verbal cues. With this in mind, then, it's sensible for you to make any changes that you feel would improve your use of body language in small – rather than big – steps. Doing this means that you'll avoid mishaps like them thinking 'what is he (or she) staring at?' when you make a change in your use of gaze. It's also worth remembering that sometimes changing a small aspect of your body language can make a big difference to the effectiveness of its use.

You'll find more information on body language in *Instant Manager: Body Language*.

Summary

Most of what you communicate to other people in your line-of-sight communication uses body language. There seems to be evidence that doing this is an innate or 'hard wired' potentiality for all human beings. It is certainly something that you start to do at a very early age – before you learn to speak – and then continue to practise and refine it throughout the rest of your life.

You do that because your use of body language

● overcomes the limitations that words sometimes have
● gives you an additional and separate communication channel.

But using body language does have its downside. For when you do that you also:

● hint at, signal or even express your inner feelings
● give messages that are often seen to be more genuine than your spoken messages
● often express or hint at feelings that are inappropriate to the place or situation that you're in; that are beyond the boundaries of 'social etiquette'.

The science of body language tells you that it involves your use of hand, arm, leg, head and eye movements, your posture and its changes, your use of gaze and facial expressions (Kinesics) and your use of distance and spacing (Proxemics), body contact and touching (Tacesics) and body appearance. Among these, gestures, facial expressions, touch, posture, your use of the space around you and your use of touch are the more significant.

Understanding the how and why of body language is worth the effort. For not only will it improve your day-to-day communications, it'll also contain the potential to improve the quality of your life. Tips towards doing that include:

1. Being body conscious
2. Acting unaffectedly
3. Being body positive
4. Taking one step at a time.

INSTANT TIP

Get out of the habit of crossing your arms or legs and get into the habit of having eye contact – but without staring.

How would you like to…?

When you attempt to persuade others, what you do is try to get them to change their minds about something. But, for the successful workplace communicator, the outcome of this persuasion isn't just about a change of mind or attitude. For it's also, and often more importantly, about a change in the way things are done – a change in behaviour. In order to achieve this you're going to have to not only communicate effectively, you're also going to have to use a different sort of persuasion. This persuasion is honest – rather than manipulative or coercive – and is done **with** rather than **to** another.

Persuasion

We are all – whether we realise it or not – immersed in a stream of persuasion. It's all around us, all of the time. The newspapers and magazines we read, the television programmes we watch, the radio programmes we listen to and the adverts that catch our eye or ear – they're all part of this never-ending flow of persuasion. It's a stream that's rich in attempts to get you to buy this or that product, to hazard this or that action, to believe this or that statement, or to accept this or that assertion.

All of this is, at its core, a form of influence. But it's a rather special and specific form. For not only is this influence a form of communication in itself, it's also a sort of influence that relies on communication to achieve its end. This happens, as the Oxford English Dictionary tells you, when you '*induce or win over (a person) to an act or course of action*'; when you '*draw the will of (another) to something, by inclining his judgement or desire to it*' or when you '*prevail upon, or urge successfully, someone to do something*'.

Acquiring a real and effective ability to do this – to persuade – is a key step for all managers. For the workplaces of our organisations are no longer the feudal domains of the Olympian autocrats of yesteryear. Here, in the twenty-first century, you work *with* rather than command your co-workers and you seek to empower them rather than dominate them. All of this should tell you that acquiring and developing the ability to persuade is a key step on the road to becoming an effective and successful workplace communicator. But in order to understand how persuasion works you'll need to start by taking a look at what's called the 'influence spectrum'.

The influence spectrum

Influencing somebody isn't a monochromatic act. There's a diverse range of ways that you and your co-workers use to influence each other. When you think about this you'll soon realise that the range of the ways that you can use to influence those around you looks like that shown in Figure 4.1:

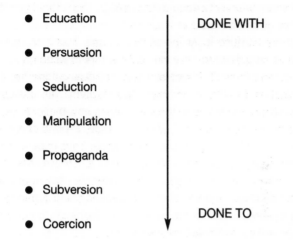

Figure 4.1: The influence spectrum

When you look at this spectrum of influence you'll see that it has, at its extremes, two very different sorts of influence process:

- **Co-operative** processes – these are done *with* people, as in education or training
- **Coercive** processes – these are done *to* people, as in forcing or compelling someone to do something.

Examples of these that you'll find in your workplace include disciplinary procedures – that are done *to* people, and training – which can only be effective if done *with* people. Probe further and look at the intentions of those processes and you'll find some more differences. For discipline is punitive or punishing while effective training is about growth and development. But these extremes of the influence spectrum also differ in the ways that they act upon us as individuals. For example, training, at its core, is about offering people the opportunity to acquire knowledge. Once that knowledge is acquired, it can be used in ways that are autonomous – that is, as you choose to use it. At the other extreme, however, coercing people or forcing them to do what you want them to do gives them little or no opportunity to exercise their individual autonomy. You'll say things like *'Do this – or else!'* leaving them with little or no individual choice about what they do. When you think about this, you'll realise that this autonomy about how you respond changes as you move through this spectrum of influence. Your experience will tell you that it is high at the 'done-with' end and low at the 'done-to' end. But all of the influence processes in this spectrum – including seduction, manipulation, propaganda and subversion – are used to some effect wherever you find people. But, in the long term, none are as significant as persuasion.

Persuasion – straight or twisted?

Take another look at the influence spectrum in Figure 4.1 and you'll see that persuasion is towards the 'done-with' end. This means that, to be effective, it – persuasion – has to have a high level of acceptance of your individual independence or autonomy.

Some of you may find this surprising.

For persuasion is often seen as unethical, unsavoury, even underhand and manipulative. It's usually associated with your being seduced away from what you really want. You are persuaded – 'despite your better judgement' as is often said – to do or to accept something.

But, in reality, persuasion is a very different animal. For, to be both effective and long lasting, this persuasion has to be based upon respect for the autonomy of the individual that you are attempting to persuade. As a result, when you use this sort of persuasion, you will need to accept that people are free to decide things for themselves. Once you accept this, a whole raft of actions that are based on domination, bullying and coercion of any kind, propaganda and, even that grand old standby of our interpersonal relationships, manipulation, become unacceptable. But that's not all – for if you really think this through you'll find that it means that, when you accept the autonomy of an individual, you – as a manager – can no longer fall back upon the authority of your role to ensure compliance or gain acceptance.

For many managers this is a big step to take.

But if you're going to be a successful communicator – it's a must-do step. For it means that persuasion is *not* something that is done *to* someone else but something that is undertaken *with* them. Real persuasion is a complex two-way process in which the role boundaries of all involved become blurred and viewpoints change. It's also a process that, as you'll now see, has four fundamental principles.

The four fundamentals

Put some more detail onto what for many of you will be a new vision of this process of persuasion and you'll soon find the Four Fundamental Principles of Persuasion. These tell you that:

- **One:** you must recognise that persuasion is an act of *communication* – and that, as you saw earlier in this book, means that it is a shared two-way process.
- **Two:** you must also recognise that persuasion is a *conscious act* that respects the autonomy of everyone involved – unlike coercion, manipulation or dominance.

- **Three:** you need to acknowledge that the desired outcome of persuasion is a *change in a persuadee's attitude* – a change that you hope will bring about different behaviour.
- **Four:** you need to accept and be conscious of the fact that the roles of *persuader* and *persuadee* are *not mutually exclusive* – and that the attitudes of both may change during the process.

So, now that you're clear about those Four Fundamental Principles, let's take a look at the where and why of this sort of persuasion.

The where and why of persuasion

When you think about persuasion you'll soon realise that it happens – or tries to happen – a lot wherever you find people. It seems to be an integral part of all our lives. As a result, the range of what might be called 'persuasive situations' is enormous. Some, but by no means all, of these occur in the workplace. One way of trying to bring some sort of structure to this diversity is to look at these in terms of their actual or potential outcomes.

When you do this you'll find that these are about:

- confirming existing attitudes or
- changing those attitudes or
- shaping or creating a new set of attitudes.

These outcomes are, of course, quite different from each other and, not surprisingly, we take different routes to get to them. For example, let's imagine that you're trying to persuade a co-worker to take on a new task. The way that you do that will take account of whether they have or haven't prior experience of this sort of task. That is to say you'll persuade them in one way if they had a prior experience of that sort of task and you'll persuade them in another way if they hadn't experienced the task before. What you'll be doing here is trying to create an outcome in which:

- existing attitudes are confirmed or changed – if their prior experience was, respectively, positive or negative, or
- you create new attitudes – if they had no prior experience.

You'll find out more about the ways in which you do this later in this chapter. However, all of this will only be successful if you recognise and validate the autonomy – the independence or self-managing ability – of the person that you're trying to persuade.

But there are many, many, workplace situations in which a change in attitude on its own is not enough. For what is done – behaviour – must also change. An example of this would be the introduction of a new Customer Service Programme. For this to be successful you'll need to persuade co-workers to accept both a change in attitude – such as the attitude that customer complaints are an opportunity to learn rather than a nuisance – and a new way of behaving – in which these complaints are reacted to positively rather than as irritating nuisances – are necessary.

However, very few of the workplace situations in which you'll use your persuasion consist of blank sheets. You'll find that, for a whole variety of reasons, the people that you are trying to persuade come with some sort of 'baggage' or prior experiences and attitudes towards the outcome that you desire. These can be positive – in which case your aim would be to confirm these existing positive attitudes – or negative – in which case your aim would be to create a change in attitudes. Either way it's important that you acknowledge and accept this prior experience and knowledge.

Now you'll take a look at the ways that persuasion can take place.

Persuasive overtures

By now you've probably begun to realise that persuasion is a process that's not as simple or as straightforward as it might appear at first glance. When you start to look at the 'how' of persuasion you'll find that this complexity increases. For doing that brings in its train questions such as 'who is persuading who?' and 'has this happened before?'

For example, you know from your own experience that persuasion is used to exert influence:

- between individuals – as between you and a member of your team, or
- between an organisation and an individual – as between a political party and you.

While each of these has very different characteristics and modes of operation, they are, at their core, identical. In this chapter you'll initially focus on the how of the persuasion that takes place between you and the people that you meet and work with in your workplaces and then, later, on the persuasions that you, as a manager, have to exert on behalf of your organisation.

One to one

We all have an enormous repertoire of experiences in this area – after all, we've been trying to persuade other people for most of our lives! We met it in childhood when our parents tried to persuade us to eat our greens – because they're 'good for us' – and our exposure to it has continued through the rest of our lives. We persuade others and are persuaded by them in an ongoing continuum of persuasive activity – activity that encompasses almost every aspect of our lives. When you think about those experiences you'll realise that the ways in which you respond to the persuasive ploys of others will be influenced by:

- whether you know the person who's trying to persuade you
- what sort of a relationship you have with them
- whether they control the potential penalties or rewards.

Put simply, you'll react differently to the persuasive overtures of a salesperson that you haven't met before and who is trying to sell you something that you don't really need and the persuasions of a boss who has the power to promote you. Equally, the ways and means of their persuasion will be different.

Take a look at Table 4.1 on page 68 and see how many of the ways and means of persuasion you can recognise.

In the workplace, however, the ways and means of this persuasion are subtly different. For example, those who you seek to persuade – or who seek to persuade you – may be in positions of power in your organisation. As such they will have power or authority over you. As a result, the persuasive strategy that you adopt towards them or the responses that you will have to their persuasive overtures will be different – they will be coloured by and take into account that authority. You may also find yourself being persuaded by – or trying to persuade – people with very real expert knowledge about the issue in hand and the ways that you act and react in this process of persuasion must take that expertise into account.

These factors – and others – can make a difference to the ways and means that you use to persuade others. But, however it's done, to be successful that persuasion must start from and continue to be rooted in the Four Fundamentals that tell you that persuasion is:

- an act of *communication*, i.e. a shared two-way process.
- a *conscious act* that respects the autonomy of everyone involved
- an act that aims to generate *changes in attitude*

Table 4.1: The ways and means of persuasion

We persuade each other by:

- **Pledging something** – like a reward, as in *'I'll see you all right'*, or a penalty, as in *'I'll have to reduce your bonus.'*

- **Displaying access to knowledge** – either in positive ways, as in *'Keep that up and you'll get promoted'*, or in negative ways, as in the infamous *'If you don't stop that you'll go blind.'*

- **Preconditioning** – as when we ask how the wife or husband and kids are before asking someone to change shifts or when we tell her she's got a bonus and then ask her to move to the Glasgow office.

- **Appealing to his or her feelings about his or herself** – as in *'You'll feel better (or worse) if you do (or don't do) this.'*

- **Attributing higher qualities** – to those who comply or lower qualities to those who don't, as in *'A mature person would agree'* or *'Only a childish person would disagree.'*

- **Invoking indebtedness** – real or imagined – as in *'You owe me one.'*

- **Appealing to an ethical stance** – as in *'It's not right to let them do this.'*

- **Appealing to their self-esteem** – as in *'People will think more of you if you agree'* or *'People will think less of you if you disagree.'*

- **Appealing to their concern or regard for others** – as in *'You'll really help us all if you agree.'*

- an act in which the roles of *persuader* and *persuadee* are *not mutually exclusive*.

Remember these and you'll find that your persuasions will be done *with* someone – rather than *to* them. It's also worth making sure that your persuasion:

- is clearly expressed, and well organised
- uses examples – they reach people while figures bore or frighten them
- shows that it's been done before
- stresses your positives but doesn't lie about or hide the negatives
- promises rewards – they generate positive results while penalties lead to negativity and nothing leads to nothing.

It's also worth remembering that research tells us that we are most easily persuaded by people that:

- we like or respect
- have power over us
- who are willing to do 'tit for tat' deals with us.

Organisational persuasion

Organisations often have to persuade people. The range of people involved in these persuasions is enormous. They can, for example, be representatives of regulatory authorities, officers of the law, judges, investment brokers, bankers, officers of insurance companies, suppliers, customers and, of course, employees. However, in this chapter, you'll only be looking at the sort of persuasion that takes place between you as an employee and the organisation that you work for.

The first thing to grasp here is that this organisation and you have different needs. For example, all organisations have a structure. This structure enables them to integrate and co-ordinate the efforts of the people that they employ and to focus these efforts toward the achievement of the organisation's goals. In the modern workday world there are quite a number of factors that exert significant influences on the nature of that structure. Technology, the marketplace, the size of the organisation, its history and, above all, its people – all of these are important. Get that structure right and an organisation is able to respond effectively and quickly to external threats and dangers and cope with a changing and complex world.

But your needs – as an individual – are different.

For not only do you need security – against deprivation in all its forms – you also need opportunities. But these aren't just any old sorts of opportunity – they must be the sort of opportunity that enables you to voluntarily commit your own efforts towards goals and targets that are personally meaningful. Above all, you need the freedom to grow and develop – even if this is in conflict with the goals or needs of the organisation. The conflicts between your needs and the needs of the organisation that employs you are obvious and real. You meet them every day of your working life and their tensions are, sadly, commonplace. It is these tensions that cause you to change employers, jobs and sometimes even careers.

Most organisations, however, are not insensitive to this dilemma.

They want to move out of this apparent deadlock and the way that they do this is to persuade you, as an employee, to accept a compromise. As an employee you will be subject to that compromise but as a manager you may also be asked to act as an agent of the organisation that you work for. In this role you will take part in the negotiations and discussions that take place around the generation of this compromise.

Broadly speaking, the ways that organisations use to persuade employees pivot around three quite different aspects of your working life. These are:

- the rewards that you get for working
- the value that you place on the organisation's goals, and
- the compatibility of your individual goals and needs and those of the organisation.

With the first two of these – those associated with rewards and organisational goals – the persuasion that takes place is primarily, but not exclusively, one-way. It is the organisation that seeks to persuade you. In the third and last one – that associated with goal compatibility – the persuasion that takes place acts in both directions. This is the one where the persuasion is true persuasion – it is mutual and two-way.

Money, money, money

In this, the first of the ways that organisations use to persuade you, the focus is on the rewards that the organisation gives you in return for your labour or effort. The primary reward is, of course, money but goods or services such as subsidised cars, travel to work, canteens, gym or health club membership as well as health insurance, access to free holiday accommodation or travel, or discounted company products or services can also be given. In return you are expected to revise and sometimes relinquish your personal goals and rules – in favour of the organisation's goals and rules. The persuasion that takes place in order to achieve this outcome is in one direction only – from the organisation to the individual – and the benefits offered are, in the beginning, a job and subsequently, money and perks.

Goals and glory

In this, the second way that organisations use, you are persuaded, as an employee, to value activities that help the organisation to achieve its goals. The rewards given for doing this are two-fold. They are:

- money, goods or services, and
- social prestige.

So, if you sell the most widgets or provide the best customer service, you'll not only get bonuses you'll also become *'Salesman of the Month"* or *'Employee of the Week'*. This sort of persuasion is also essentially a one-way process. The organisation persuades, the individual is persuaded. The organisation expects you as an individual to acquiesce or accede to the needs of the organisation. The role of manager can be important in this process, providing examples of how to behave, acting as an interpreter of the organisation's goals and rules, and providing a model to be emulated and by so doing achieve further rewards.

Compatibility

In this, the third and final way that organisations use to persuade you, the persuasion process changes from being one that acts solely in one direction – from organisation to individual – to become one which acts in both directions – from organisation to individual and vice versa. But that is not the only difference, for when an organisation invokes this type of persuasion it also accepts the validity of the individual's rules, goals and needs. Once it does that, then it must operate in such a way as to ensure that not only are its own goals, in themselves, rewarding to the individuals who are paid to achieve them but also that these goals provide for and allow the concurrent pursuit of the individual's personal goals.

Organisations like this are rare and hard to find. But they do encourage high levels of self-autonomy among their employees; a situation that leads to high levels of trust, support and co-operation. As such these are the true homes of the effective workplace communicator.

To find out how you're coming along use the Persuasion Self-evaluation Questionnaire (Table 4.2) at the end of the chapter to check what your persuasion rating is.

Summary

In this chapter you've seen that persuasion is one of the ways that you influence others. But true persuasion, unlike some of the other ways of influencing each other, is done *with* a person rather than *to* them.

As such it's also:

- an act of communication
- a shared two-way process
- a conscious act
- an act by which attitudes on both sides can be changed.

Persuasion can be used to:

- confirm existing attitudes or
- change those attitudes or
- create new attitudes.

But persuasion isn't just about changing attitudes; it also aims to change the way things are done – behaviours. Persuasion can take place between:

- individuals, and
- organisations and individuals.

Good persuasion involves:

- clarity and organisation
- use of examples and evidence
- stressing positives
- rewards.

INSTANT TIP

To be persuasive you have to be believable – which means that you have to be credible – which, in the end, means that you have to be truthful.

Table 4.2: Persuasion Self-evaluation Questionnaire

Ring the number that's closest to the way you do it. Then add up your total score.

Preparation

I'm clear about the outcome that I want to achieve	**1 2 3 4 5 6 7**	I'm not sure why I'm doing this
I'm clear about who I want to persuade	**1 2 3 4 5 6 7**	I'm not sure who I ought to talk to
I've found out about their background	**1 2 3 4 5 6 7**	I've no idea what their background is
I'm clear about whether I intend to create, confirm or change attitudes	**1 2 3 4 5 6 7**	What do you mean?

Doing it

I'm prepared to modify my desired outcome	**1 2 3 4 5 6 7**	I will persuade them to do what I want
I'll listen to what they say	**1 2 3 4 5 6 7**	I expect them to listen to me
This is something that we are doing together	**1 2 3 4 5 6 7**	I'm doing it to them

SCORING

If your total score comes to 21 or less then you appear to be persuading well. Scores of 28 and above indicate that you are having some problems.

Do you want to do a deal?

The act of negotiating appears everywhere. It has a history that's probably as long as humankind's and the nature and span of its involvement in human affairs is encyclopaedic. Some say that the ability to negotiate is **the** truly human characteristic. For the effective and successful workplace communicator, negotiating is an enabling process – rather than a win–lose battle – and one that enables all involved to achieve real wins. This chapter takes a look at the ways in which you can negotiate and bargain and finds the linkages to and benefits for the process of focused and effective communication.

Negotiations in the workplace

In the world at large, your negotiations can be about anything – the price of a house or a car, the detail of a service, the value of a holiday or a computer, who gets the coffee or who pays for the next round of drinks. We even negotiate, some say, about love and affection. Yet, in all of these and the many, many other negotiations that you'll get involved in, you'll start when you see that someone has something that you want; something that you are prepared to exchange for another thing that you value. You'll finish when you and that other person agree an exchange involving these. Some of us do this well – and get what we want for less than we were prepared to pay. Others do it badly – and find themselves giving up something they valued for less than they had thought it was worth. The ways that you use to reach these agreements are never straightforward or simple. Most of us muddle through; we fall into success by accident rather than by design. Even when we achieve that success we remain unsure as to whether the other party would have paid more or we might have paid too much.

Your workplace negotiations are just as diverse as they are elsewhere. You negotiate with your boss, your co-workers, your suppliers, your contractors and your customers. These negotiations are about things like how much you get paid, how much you pay someone else, who's in charge, who decides what, how you get the information that you want or if you get the people or equipment that you need.

Some of these negotiations are formal. They take place in meeting rooms and boardrooms; they are public or organisational events, involving teams of negotiators – rather than a single individual – and draw on complex systems of rules and relationships. But the majority of negotiations that take place in your workplace are informal. They happen between you and other individuals – at the coffee machine, over the lunch table, around a desk. The ways that they are conducted have much in common with the sort of bargaining that takes place in marketplaces and street markets all over the world.

Yet these, your informal negotiations, are just as important as their formal *'set-piece'* cousins. For they occur on an hour-by-hour, day-by-day basis; they are about who will do what and when and sometimes why. They form a vitally important strand in the processes of managing and motivating individuals and teams. The ability to undertake these negotiations and do that well lies at the core of the manager's job. As such, you – as a manager – must be able to:

- recognise these negotiations for what they are
- conduct them effectively, and
- recognise that effective communication is a key factor in their success.

But, as you'll soon see, these negotiations are just one of the ways that get used to resolve workplace conflicts.

Conflict, conflict and conflict

A conflict or a clash of interests arises when someone else has something that you want or gets in the way of you achieving what you want to achieve. But this conflict doesn't come about because you're selfish or greedy. For we all have drives and needs and what we do, or don't do, is strongly influenced by these. When your needs can't be answered from your own resources then you seek to have them answered from elsewhere. This usually involves you being in competition with other people – after all, they too have drives and needs – and it is this competition that leads you into conflict with them. This sort of conflict is common in the workplace. It occurs between individuals, teams, departments and sections and can be about almost anything. But it's often about such things as who uses or possesses scarce resources – such as money or skilled personnel – or who has the most power and influence – as when an individual or department is 'top-dog' when it comes to making decisions about the organisation's future. However, these workplace conflicts can also have their roots in your individual likes, dislikes and prejudices.

The need to resolve these conflicts effectively and quickly can make considerable demands on a manager's time. But resolve them he or she must.

Conflict resolution

Given the widespread nature of conflict you shouldn't be surprised when you find that a number of ways have developed for coping with or resolving it. Here are five basic ways:

- **Avoid it** or **Ignore it and it will go away**
- **Compete to win**
- **Give up and give in**
- **Form partnerships**
- **Find a middle course** or **Negotiate.**

Where and when you use these will depend upon the circumstances and situations that you find yourself in. For example, the 'Ignore it and it will go away' approach is usually best used with conflicts that have trivial outcomes or conflicts for which the cost of resolution outweighs the benefits. But the 'I'm going to win, you're going to lose' approach – with its strong emotional appeal – has significant long-term limitations. For this approach invites hostility and winning every time is very difficult if not impossible! The opposite extreme – 'Giving in and giving up' – can help you cope with conflict when you are in the wrong or when you need to minimise your losses when losing. It can also be used to 'keep the peace'. The two remaining approaches – 'Forming partnerships' and the 'Middle course' approach – have much in common. For they both strive to create win–win solutions to conflict. However, the differences between them are significant. For when forming partnerships you need to learn about each other's needs and wants, gain commitment by creating consensus and attempt to maintain your relationships by working through interfering feelings. Doing this – desirable as it is – takes time, and time can be of the essence. For this reason it is often the 'Middle course' or, as it's usually called, the 'Negotiation' approach to resolving conflict that will give you the best results. It's an approach that is most effective when you treat the person that you're negotiating with as an equal.

It can act in ways that help you to resolve apparently incompatible goals and to generate appropriate solutions when under time pressure. When you use the negotiation approach to resolving conflict you forge links with others; practical, pragmatic links that are about joint success, links that you can use in the future. Effective communication is key to doing all of this.

What is negotiation?

When you look up the verb *'to negotiate'* in a dictionary there are a number of definitions. You'll find, for example, that to negotiate can mean *'to discuss a matter with a view to some settlement or compromise'* or *'to hold communication or conference (with another) for the purpose of arranging some matter by mutual agreement'*. Other definitions tell us about the transaction of business, the settlement of issues by discussion and bargaining, attempts to come to terms and conferring and seeking agreement.

You've already seen that negotiations can take place everywhere and can be about anything. When you probe further into this rich diversity you'll find that:

- the act of negotiating always involves two, or more, people
- these people can act:
  - for themselves, or
  - for others
- negotiations can be formal or informal
- most, though not all, negotiations are face to face.

You'll also find that:

- negotiation has conflict – between your needs and those of others – as its starting point, and

● when successful, negotiation has a jointly agreed decision as its outcome.

But that's not all that you'll discover.

You'll also find that, when they are successful, these negotiations have outcomes that:

● are about your future, and
● are agreed by all involved.

What all of this begins to tell you is that negotiation isn't a win–lose battle of wits. It's a way of resolving your differences with others and jointly identifying and agreeing what you and others will do in the future.

So how do you do carry out this process of negotiation?

How do you negotiate?

Most people think of negotiation as a process that just involves haggling over the price of some goods or service. But, in fact, negotiation involves far more than that. In reality it's a complex process with several distinct and separate steps or stages. However, the first step will always be that of preparing yourself.

Preparation

This preparation starts with you being clear about what you do – and don't – want as an outcome. But that's not all. For it also involves you in finding out about the person that you'll be negotiating with – what sort of a person are they and how are they likely to negotiate with you? You may also need to think about the where and when of the negotiations – factors that in formal negotiations can be the subject of negotiations themselves. If your negotiations are about really big issues, this preparation can take up quite a lot of time and effort. In large organisations, such as corporations or governments, it's often undertaken by support teams.

But, however long it takes, this preparation is always about the detail of the approach to and the content of what's called the 'bargaining zone'. Preparing well is important, for it can make the difference between success and failure at the negotiating table. Table 5.1 is a checklist that you can use for your preparation.

Table 5.1: Preparation checklist

---

1. Background

What are the issues on which negotiation will take place?

What are the historic facts and figures?

Who are you negotiating with?

What's known about their skills, experience, background and values?

What's known about their needs and wants?

Where will the negotiation take place?

When will the negotiation take place?

2. Objectives

What do you want to achieve?

What is the best that can be realistically hoped for?

What is the worst that will be settled for?

What is known about the opponent's position on the above?

Table 5.1: *Continued*

---

3. Bargaining strengths and weaknesses

What are:

- Your strengths – technical, price, cost, cash flow, experience, time, etc?
- Your weaknesses – technical, price, cost, cash flow, experience, time, etc?

What information do you have about the other person's strengths and weaknesses?

Once you've answered all these questions then – and only then – are you ready to move on to the next step, where you'll take some decisions about the conduct – or strategy and tactics – of your negotiation.

Strategy and tactics

Strategy and tactics often get mixed up or confused.

In its simplest form, strategy is about large-scale, long-term and final outcomes while tactics are about small-scale and short-term interim issues. For example, the strategic decisions about a journey will be about where the journey is from and to, the mode of travel – car, train, plane or boat – and when the journey takes place. The tactical decisions of the journey will be about the detail of the route and the nature or style of the interactions with traffic or fellow travellers on the journey.

In your negotiations, your strategic decisions are about the outcome and pace of the bargaining process while your tactical decisions are about the detail of how you react to this or that ploy or offer.

Both of these – to be successful – need to take into account the factors that you will have identified during your preparation. They must be chosen with care and with due regard for the outcome that you desire. But, above all, they must be effective.

However, your negotiating strategy must also recognise that the person that you negotiate with and you yourself have interests that are shared and in common. This sort of strategy is really a search – a search for agreements, agreements that are mutually beneficial, that satisfy the needs of both parties. It is also a strategy that requires high levels of trust between negotiators, a willingness to exchange information and an ability to compromise.

Operating such a strategy isn't easy.

But when you examine the choices that you have you'll soon realise that there is only one alternative to such a strategy. This is a strategy of non-communication, of limited trust, of conflicting interests, of limited and 'tailored' information exchange and, in the long run, of limited effectiveness. Faced with such a choice being effective in your communication, trusting and open is not only the right choice – it's also a more effective use of your communication skills as well as being in your long-term interests.

Negotiations

You've completed your preparation, got together all the information that you need and decided what strategy and tactical approach you'll follow. Now, at last, you can begin your negotiation. But even this, the act of negotiation, has its own set of steps and stages – as you'll now see:

STAGE ONE: In this, the initial stage of your negotiation, you will act quite formally. You and the other person will tell each other – sometimes at length – that your goals are probably incompatible, that you don't really need to reach an agreement or that your enthusiasm for achieving an outcome is low and that you intend to stand firm. All of this is actually a bit of a ritual; one designed to prepare the ground so that any future concessions seem greater than they are or that any threatened breakdowns are seen as real. When you negotiate for your organisation you will also stress the representative nature of your roles – in order to depersonalise the negotiation.

STAGE TWO: In this, the second stage of your negotiation, you'll spend a lot of time trying to find pathways to possible agreement. But you will make sure that these are seen as *possible* future options rather than concrete commitments or agreements. You'll do this as an individual and you will stress things like the need to 'think it over' or the difficulties in gaining agreement from others – such as the rest of the team – before you can commit yourself. The way that you'll behave in this stage will be much more informal and 'unofficial' than the first stage. Nevertheless, this is the stage that prepares the ground for the third and final stage.

STAGE THREE: In this, the third and final stage, you'll return to a more formal way of behaving; one that takes the possibilities that you identified in the previous stage and attempts to convert one of these into the concrete reality of an agreement. Your route from option to agreement is marked by offers, counter-offers, decisions, disagreements and, hopefully and finally, agreement. But this doesn't always happen and you may find yourself having to face the fact that the gap is too big to be bridged – at this time. In this event, the outcome can still be an agreement. But, rather than being about the detail of your future joint actions, it's an agreement about the reasons why that hasn't come to pass. But even this isn't a failure. For this sort of agreement prepares you for agreement in the future – next time or when the market or your needs have changed.

The preparations that you had undertaken earlier contribute to all of these stages. They tell you, for example, how far you can go in pushing for an agreement to your advantage, they tell you when to stand firm or when to concede. They also, most importantly, enable you to identify the boundaries of your bargaining zone.

The bargaining zone

The act of bargaining occurs worldwide – in marketplaces, on street corners, in the jungles of Africa or in the deserts of Arabia. In all of these places and many, many more, you'll find people bargaining. When they do this they are trying to find a way of agreeing about an act of exchange. Bargaining is about haggling, wrangling, dealing or bartering – and it also lies at the core of your negotiations.

In your preparation you will have identified what are, for you, the acceptable limits of this core area – the Bargaining Zone; you'll have explored its contours during the second stage of your negotiations and you will create its *raison d'être* – a bargain – in the third and final stage.

All of this will demand much of you as a negotiator. You'll need to be able to use negotiating skills and use them in ways that are consistent and credible. The momentary slip of impatience, the apparent anger of an *'Of course I mean that!'* reaction can ruin the efforts of many hours of work.

When you look at the Bargaining Zone (Figure 5.1) you can see that its boundaries are set by the levels of the buyer's maximum offer and the seller's minimum price. These represent the ideal outcomes for the buyer and seller respectively and you can also see that, for the Bargaining Zone to exist, the buyer's maximum offer must exceed the seller's minimum price. If this doesn't happen, that is if the buyer's maximum offer is less than the seller's minimum price, then the Bargaining Zone doesn't exist and a deal or outcome can't be achieved. What happens in a successful negotiation is that the buyer's offer and the seller's price will converge at the same value. The process of bargaining that leads to this is one that demands much skill, stamina and experience from you. But that's not all – for in order to achieve success in your negotiations you'll need, as you'll now see, to behave in certain ways.

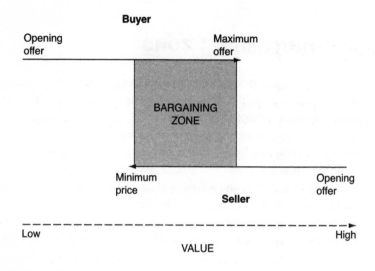

Figure 5.1: The Bargaining Zone

Negotiating – do's and don'ts

Effective negotiators are rare animals. Most of us muddle through our negotiations and achieve success by accident – rather than the focused exercise of skill. Those that we meet in these negotiations are often as ill prepared as we are – or hell bent on winning at our cost. But when you do meet an effective and focused negotiator, things are different. For the intent of such a negotiator is not to win at your cost but to ensure that both of you arrive at a mutually acceptable agreement – that both of you win.

So how do they achieve this?

You've already seen one of the key elements of this success – preparation. Now you're going to see another key element – the way that effective negotiators do – and don't – behave in face-to-face negotiations.

Negotiating don'ts

The sorts of behaviour that skilled negotiators don't indulge in include irritating the other negotiator, slowing the negotiation down, diverting its focus or implying that it's a win–lose rather than a win–win negotiation.

For example, skilled negotiators avoid using:

- **Irritators** – which are words and phrases that are commonly used by you and I but that have negligible persuasive effect and do cause irritation.
- **Immediate counter proposals** – that occur when a proposal by one negotiator is immediately followed by an alternative or counter proposal from the other negotiator.
- **Patterns of related defence and attack** – these often occur when negotiations become emotionally heated. An attack by one negotiator will lead to a heated defence – or counter attack – by the other. This, in its turn, is perceived as an attack and so induces an attack response from the first negotiator, and so on. What often occurs is that the intensity of the interchanges spirals upwards, often leading to one or other negotiator storming out. If it sounds familiar it's because we all behave like this when we get upset – so stay cool.
- **Dilution by argument** – this happens when you use too many reasons to support your case. Instead of adding to that case these provide the other negotiator with more material for dispute or show up your potential weaknesses.

Take a look in Table 5.2 for examples of these and other negotiating don'ts.

Table 5.2: Unskilled negotiating behaviour

Irritators
Management Negotiator: *'I believe that we are making an offer which, given the current state of the market, is not just fair but also downright generous.'*

Immediate counter proposals
Negotiator A: *'I suggest that we have a coffee before we drive over to John's.'*
Negotiator B: *'How about having coffee when we get there?'*

Defence/attack patterns
Negotiator A: *'What you are asking is ridiculous. If you had any understanding of basic economics you would know what I'm talking about.'*
Negotiator B: *'If you had any understanding of people then you wouldn't be proposing such an arrangement.'*
Negotiator A: *'In all of my 20 years as a manager I've never met such an unco-operative attitude as yours.'*
Negotiator B: *'I don't care about your 20 years' experience ...'*
etc. etc. etc.

Dilution by argument
Management Negotiator: *'I believe that this proposal for revised working hours is the right proposal because it enables the company to be more responsive to its customers, makes better use of the part-time female workers and solves our car parking problems.'*
Union Negotiator: *'It's funny that you should mention the car parking – I've had it mind to talk to you about that for some time.'*

Signalling disagreement
Negotiator: *'I disagree with your proposals because they don't go far enough to meet my needs and will cost me too much to implement.'*

Negotiating do's

When you look at the ways that skilled negotiators behave you find that they use:

- **Behaviour signals or labels** that give prior or advance notice of the oncoming actions or behaviour. They can also be used to slow down the negotiation – thus giving time for thought – or to keep the negotiation at a more formal level when there is a danger of tempers rising. They are, however, rarely used to signal disagreement.
- **Reason/disagreement patterns** that start with a statement of explanation that then leads to a statement of disagreement. Most of us do it the other way round, i.e. disagreement first, rather than reasons or explanations.
- **Testing and summarising questions and statements** that prevent misunderstanding and promote clarity.
- **Asking for information** that encourages the other negotiator to share more of his or her information. It also helps with control of negotiations and can provide time to think while the other negotiator is occupied in generating the answer.
- **Statements about feelings** – skilled negotiators use these to give the other negotiator more information about feelings and motives.

Take a look at Table 5.3 on page 92 for examples of these.

Table 5.3: Skilled negotiating behaviour

Signalling behaviour
Negotiator: *'I wonder if I might ask a question. How many times has this happened?'*

Not signalling disagreement
Negotiator: *'Because your proposals don't go far enough to meet my needs and will cost me too much to implement, I cannot agree to what you are suggesting.'*

Testing and summarising
Negotiator: *'If I can summarise where I think we've got to – you have said that you will be able to accept our revised proposals about pay structures but have difficulty with the current working hours proposals. Have I understood you correctly?'*

Implementation concern
Negotiator: *'I would like to ask some more questions about the new duty rota and how it will work, since in the end my members will have to work this new rota.'*

Seeking information
Negotiator: *'At what size of order would I get a bigger discount?'*

Statements about feelings
Negotiator: *'We've been talking now for almost an hour and I'm beginning to feel some concern about the big differences that there still are between us.'*

Summary

In this chapter you've seen that negotiation is a very common way of resolving conflict. At its core, negotiating is a joint decision-making process about future actions. Successful and effective negotiating needs:

- real and effective communication skills
- thorough careful preparation
- a thoughtful and well-considered choice of strategy.

The process of negotiation is complex and contains stages that are about:

- ritualised position identification
- informal search for agreement
- finalisation and formalisation of agreement.

Effective negotiators behave in ways that involve signalling oncoming behaviours, preceding disagreement by reasons, testing and summarising, seeking information and expressing feelings.

INSTANT TIP

If you are planning on doing business with someone in the future, think long term and don't be too tough in your negotiations with them.

06

Can I explain?

The act of explaining is a key component in the tool bag of the successful workplace communicator. However, few of us are born with a natural aptitude for explaining. In this chapter you'll take a look, firstly, at the what and why of explaining and then, secondly, at the ways and means in which that explaining can, and does, happen. By the end of the chapter you'll have a good idea of the contribution that explaining can make to both the quality and success of your workplace communication.

Explaining – the what and why

Explaining is a process that has, at its core, the act of giving information. As such, it is, as you saw in Chapter 1, a 'mainstream' activity when it comes to the process of communication. But that's not all that emerges when you take a look at the process of explaining. For it's also:

- a very commonly used process, and
- a process that's extraordinarily versatile.

For your explanations can be about almost anything. They can, for example, be about:

- facts, or
- opinions, or
- theories and hypotheses, or
- conclusions or deductions.

This diversity continues to be present when you come to look at the desired end-points or outcomes of your explanations. For when you explain you're usually aiming to answer questions such as:

- why will, does or did something happen?, or
- how will, does or did something happen?, or even
- when or where will, does, or did something happen?

But, despite all of this multiplicity, the people that study these things tell us that explanations do have a number of characteristics in common. For they often contain:

- statements based on logic – such as 'because of this we have concluded that ...'
- cause/effect relationships – using words and phrases such as 'then', 'as a consequence' and 'so then'
- statements about time relationships – using words such as 'first', 'then', 'following' and 'finally'.

The language that you use in your explanations often adopts or uses:

- the present tense – such as 'are', 'turns' or 'happens'
- action related verbs – such as 'falls', 'rises' or 'changes'
- non-human participants – such as 'the sea' or 'the computer'
- conjunctions – such as 'when', 'then' or ' first'.

Your explanations will also often use general nouns – such as cars, boats or birds; passive statements such as 'is saturated' or 'are changed', and pronouns – such as 'they' and 'their'.

Yet, despite this complexity, explanations are a commonly used way of communicating. So let's see if we can refine and condense some of this complexity and diversity – and generate a simpler definition of explanation.

Explaining – a definition

When you go to your dictionary and take a look at the definitions of the verb 'to explain' you'll find that there's quite a range of them. For example, you'll find that it's a verb that can mean any of these:

- *to smooth out, make smooth, take out roughness from,* or
- *to open out, unfold, spread out flat a material object,* or
- *to make plainly visible; to display.*

While some of these give you some pretty broad hints as to what explaining is about, they still don't give you a definition that's directly related to the process of communication.

So what we'll do here is to generate one for ourselves. The result – a definition that you can directly link to the process of communication – is one that tells us that the outcome of your explaining – your explanation – is:

a description of an event, process or state of affairs that attempts to illuminate or make clear its causes, context and consequences.

Now that you've got to the point where you know what an explanation is it's time to move on to take a look at the ways and means of your explanations.

Explaining – the ways and means

As you saw at the beginning of this chapter, explaining is, at its core, about communicating. When you explain you use:

- written language, or
- spoken language together with non-verbal communication or body language.

But this isn't really an 'either/or' situation. For you can give somebody an explanation in the form of a letter or a report and then support that written explanation with spoken words – as in a telephone conversation – or spoken words and non-verbal communication – as in a presentation. In this book you are going to look, in more detail, at three of the more commonly used and important ways and means of that explaining. By and large, these are the ways of explaining that use:

- talk
- written material
- presentations.

Let's look at each of these in more detail.

Talk

Talking is something that we all do a lot. It's also, as you saw in Chapter 1, one of the most important ways in which we communicate. This talking is, or can be, extraordinarily versatile – it'll enable you persuade, influence, instruct, inform and, of course, explain. As you saw in Chapter 2, a lot of this talking takes place in informal small groups and involves conversations, discussions, debates and dialogues. If you're not sure about how important these ways of talking together are then it's worth going back to Chapter 2 and checking them over again. But if you don't feel that you need to do that, do try to remember they involve small groups of people, use spoken and body language and have the potential to be highly creative.

But not all of your talking will take place in informal groups like this. For you'll also explain things to other people when you talk:

- on the telephone, or
- in a formal meeting.

So let's look at each of these in turn.

Telephone talk

When you talk face to face your words and movements begin to fall into a sort of 'dance' with each other. The rhythm, volume, speech rate and pitch of your talking, your gestures and 'micro-movements' – all of these become interwoven, harmonised. But when you talk on the telephone, things are different. Then, you're visually cut off from the person you are talking to. As a result there are no gestures, grimaces or smiles to tell you what they think of what you are saying; there are no nods or turns of the head that tell you that they can hear you. What this means is that those who hear you are free of the messages, distractions and deceits contained in your body language. Now they can focus on your voice; they 'read' the tone or pitch of it, listen to the way that you do or don't hesitate, hear the pauses in or between your sentences, and notice the speed or volume of your speech. They make use of these to deduce how you are feeling or what your attitude is toward them or the subject under discussion. So when you're explaining something over the telephone here are the key points that you need to bear in mind:

- prepare by making sure – before you make the call – that you're clear about the who, why and what of your call
- make a list of your objectives and tick them off during the call when you achieve them
- if it's a *really* important call, then it's worth thinking about getting someone to help you with a rehearsal
- start by telling them who you are and why you've called
- take and keep the initiative but pause, from time to time, to allow feedback or questions
- keep it simple
- listen when they respond – particularly when they ask questions
- make sure your answers are generous – but not excessive – and always ask if you've achieved an acceptable answer
- summarise, briefly, at the end.

Formal meetings

Meetings like this happen quite a lot in the workplace. Typically they involve four or more people coming together to carry out the formal business of the organisation. Their objectives usually include such significant issues as planning new models or products, making policy decisions, agreeing project expenditure or revising next year's budget. But that's not the only thing that these meetings manage to do. They also manage to bore the pants of most of the people who attend them!

This usually happens because they go on for too long, have too many people attending or don't have the 'right' people there. But most of the time, formal meetings like this fail because the people who attend them haven't prepared for the meeting.

Your attendance at these meetings usually comes about because of your role or job. Often you'll need to attend in order to explain your section's or team's case for, say, increased recruitment or better computers. If you're going to make sure that your explanation of the background or reasons for your proposal is effective, then there are some basic things that you've got to get 'right'. These are that you:

- make sure that:
  - your project or subject is on the agenda
  - you've sent copies of the relevant documents to all the people attending well before the meeting date
- don't speak before the chairperson invites you to and when you do:
  - speak clearly and concisely, and
  - keep your explanation brief and simple
- invite questions and be prepared to answer them
- be prepared to compromise and negotiate
- accept the meeting's decision – whatever it is – with good grace and thank the meeting – through the chairperson – for their time.

There may, however, be some subjects or projects for which your organisation may require you to prepare and give a full presentation as an explanation. Later in this chapter you'll look at the key guidelines that will enable you to do that – and do it well.

Written material

The written word has a great deal to contribute to your workplace communications and you'll explore its ways and means more fully in the next chapter. In the meantime, let's take a brief look at the benefits of using the written word for your explanation. For when you write your explanation:

- you can put more thought into your explanation than you would into a verbal explanation
- you can revise the choice of words that you use, rewriting or reshaping the text until you are satisfied
- you can express your own ideas and conclusions in your own way and without having to respond to the reader's reactions and responses
- your explanation can be easily copied and so sent to a number of people at the same time
- your explanation can be formal or informal, lengthy or brief.

Here are some guidelines to help you to write explanations that will reach your reader:

- use a title that indicates what you are writing about
- decide whether diagrams, charts or illustrations would help
- use the first paragraph to introduce the subject and define key words
- organise your writing carefully; ask yourself 'Do the ideas flow?'
- finish your writing by drawing the key points and conclusions together in a concluding paragraph
- don't use specialist terminology or 'jargon' unless it's essential and, if you do, provide a glossary

- when you think that you've finished, get someone else to read it or reread your explanation yourself pretending that you don't know anything about its subject and asking yourself the following questions:
  - does it make sense?
  - is it clear?
  - is my explanation accurate?
  - is my explanation complete?
  - will the reader be able to understand the terms and concepts?

Presentations

The presentation has become the default mode of group communication. It's become an omni-present, ever-ready event that can be about almost anything. The aims and objectives of these presentations can be to persuade, to inform, to influence and, of course, to explain. All of these are important – both to you and your employer. For they hold within them the potential to change your world of work. But achieving that, getting to the point where that potential becomes actual, can only be done when your presentations are:

- powerful
- passionate
- persuasive, and above all,
- professional.

Many, many specialist books and articles have been written with the intention of telling you how to get your presentation 'right'. In this book, however, you'll look at a basic outline of the core factors that will enable you to present your explanations effectively. This process – of getting to a presentation with the above characteristics

– is an important one. It starts with you answering the four following questions.

- Why are you giving the presentation or explanation?
- What are you going to say?
- Who are you going to say it to?
- How are you going to say it?

Let's look at how you might answer those questions.

Why are you giving a presentation or an explanation?

This is a tricky one. It's really got two parts to it – the first being 'why a presentation or an explanation?' instead of writing a letter or a report or making a telephone call – and the second being 'what's the objective of the presentation or explanation?' Your answers to the first part might include *'we need to bring all the decision makers together'* or *'we haven't got time to see everyone individually'*. In order to get the *right* answer to the second part – the one about the objective – you need to write the objective down in a single short sentence. It has to be short, concise and correct. Until you've done that you haven't a firm foundation on which to create your presentation.

What are you going to say?

The answer to this one starts the process of creating the presentation or explanation. This has three stages:

- **Generating the content** – by committing to paper in unstructured draft form *all* of the relevant information.
- **Prioritising** – by sorting that material into:
  - **musts:** essential to meet the objective
  - **shoulds:** important or valuable – but not essential
  - **coulds:** interesting – but can be left out.
- **Ordering** – by putting the sorted material into the best sequence. This can be logical, chronological or that which takes the audience from known to unknown.

Who are you going to say it to?

Your audience is very important and if you don't consider them carefully then you'll fail in your explanation. Find out all you can about them – ages, backgrounds, likes and dislikes, prejudices. Even if you've never met them you can reasonably assume that they:

- are experienced adults
- will usually – but not always – begin by being sympathetic and friendly
- will initially assume that you know your subject
- will listen – if you capture their imagination
- will respond to variety
- are easily distracted
- have memories that are helped by repetition
- lose concentration after about ten minutes
- are accessed best through their sense of sight.

How are you going to say it?

Key points here are:

- First impressions count – smile, look 'em in the eyes and have your first few sentences off pat.
- Keep in touch – don't talk at your notes or graphics, look at your audience.
- Speak naturally – use your enthusiasm, don't read out your notes.
- Appear confident and relaxed – you may not feel it but it's important that you look it.
- Avoid distractions – NO ums, ers, coughs, jangling keys or coins.
- Take care with humour – it can backfire on you and a flat joke is worse than no joke.
- Concentrate on communicating – watch your audience, look out for signs of boredom, puzzlement or distraction – and respond to them.

But that's not all there is to giving a good presentation and, here in no particular order, are some further thoughts that might help.

Openings

The way that you open your presentation is one of the features that distinguishes the excellent from the merely adequate presenter. There are many ways of doing it but in that opening sentence or two you should aim to:

- concentrate the minds of the audience on the topic of your presentation

- create impact, even excitement
- establish your authority
- introduce the subject
- arouse curiosity and involvement.

Closings

The way that you close a presentation is as important as the way that you open it. You should aim to leave the audience in one or more of these conditions:

- remembering what you've told them
- motivated to do something
- on a high note
- committed to doing something.

Audience contact

Your key task, as a presenter, is to create and maintain an environment in which the audience can assimilate all the information that you give them. In order to do this you need:

- to be in continuous contact with each member of the audience
- to use their ears and eyes to maintain that contact.

Body posture

When you're presenting, the way that you stand tells your audience quite a lot about you. So if you stand upright, straight but not rigid backed, shoulders back and in an asymmetrical posture, but not leaning on anything – then your audience will see you as relaxed and dominant and they will warm to you. If you smile and use open palm gestures, hold eye contact just a little longer than is comfortable, then they will also see you as honest.

Preparing yourself

Good presentations don't just happen. Not only do you have to prepare your material, you also have to prepare yourself. The only way that this can be done is by rehearsing. Rehearsals will help you to edit and refine both your material and the ways in which you present it. When you rehearse you will:

- have the chance to improve your material
- become more familiar with that material
- grow more confident in your delivery skills
- make your presentation smoother.

A rehearsal needs an audience – one or two people will do, preferably ones you can trust to tell you the truth – and is better done 'for real' – that is with the actual equipment you're going to use and, if at all possible, in the actual room.

Rehearsals come in four sorts:

- **Stagger-through rehearsal** – this first run-through will be disjointed with many stops and starts. Make sure someone takes notes of where it fell apart – they're very useful later.

- **Walk-through rehearsal** – this should be more fluent and also quicker – if you've sorted out the problems noted in the stagger-through rehearsal.
- **Run-through rehearsal** – this will add even more fluency and flow. For a presentation involving several presenters you may need more than one of these.
- **Final rehearsal** – this should prove that you've got it right.

Presentation equipment

Almost all of the equipment that you'll use during your presentation will be to do with your visual material. This can range from the very simple – as in a flip chart or black board – to the very sophisticated – as in computer-driven multiple-monitor systems. Whichever you use you *must* be familiar with both the equipment and its own particular set of problems before you set foot in front of your audience.

Visual aids

These need to be simple and clear. Good rules of thumb include:

- Avoid large tables with lots of figures.
- Don't use more than 30 numbers on each visual aid.
- Don't put more than 36 words and six lines on each visual aid.
- Use bullet points.
- Present your data in visual rather than numerical form.

Remember that people remember images for longer than they do words or numbers.

Voice and speech

It's not so much what you say as the way that you say it that affects the degree of contact you have with your audience. The voice is a powerful instrument and can be used to good effect if you just follow a few basic rules:

- **Use short sentences** This is not 'dumbing down' your presentation, it's recognising the fact that your audience will retain far more of what you say if it's put in 'bite-sized' pieces.
- **Be audible** Project your voice beyond the audience, it's probably better to speak too loudly rather than too quietly.
- **Be distinct** Make a conscious effort to make more use of your lips and mouth – to ensure that the way that you pronounce your words is clear and distinct.
- **Not too fast but not too slow** The speed of your speech should be:
  - slow enough for people to hear everything that you say but also
  - fast enough to ensure that they don't lose the thread. Varying the pace from time to time is good – it helps to generate that 'buzz' that keeps the audience interested.
- **Use pauses** Pauses are good – they create dramatic impact and help structure your words. Too many pauses, however, will leave your audience feeling that you're nervous.
- **Use emphasis** Emphasis is powerful weapon that can increase impact – especially when accompanied by the appropriate facial expression.
- **Use inflection** Inflection is about the way that you modulate your voice; the way that you change its pitch or tone when speaking. You'll need to do it consciously at first but it will get easier as time goes on. As you do you'll find that your audiences become more interested and alert.

Movements

Presentations need movements – just imagine what they'd be like without them! The movements that you make will be:

- dictated by external needs – such as switching the film projector on or off, turning over a flip chart or pointing to an object, or
- motivated by spontaneous feelings or thoughts, or
- unconscious.

Remember that everybody is watching you and try to make your conscious movements as fluid as you can. These show your audience that you are engaged in the task of communicating with them. These movements will support the words that you speak and often display emotion. Unconscious movements can, however, present difficulties. These are the movements that you've picked up and cultivated over the years. They are as much a part of your personality as the way that you walk or comb your hair. But when they distract the audience from what you are saying they become a problem. This happens when they are repeated frequently or are inappropriate. Your aim should be to use gesture and movement in a manner that is conscious and controlled but also supported – rather than dominated – by those unconscious gestures that make you who you are.

Doing it

These are the key issues:

- **Own the presentation** – make it reflect your preparation, your style and personality, your material, your rehearsals and your experience.

- **Be conscious** – not only of what you say but also the way in which you say it.
- **Speak with strength and clarity** – but not too fast or too slow.
- **Establish and maintain eye contact** – with everyone.
- **Use pauses and emphasis** – and vary your pitch and pace.
- **Enjoy it!**

All these ways of explaining have the potential to become major elements of your communications tool bag. But if you are going to learn to use them and allow them to contribute to your communicative ability then you'll have to deliberately expose yourself to them. You'll have to seek out and find those in your workplace who are skilful in their use and expose yourself to their rhetoric. You also have to polish your use of them. Give it a go!

Summary

In this chapter you've learnt that explaining is a key skill in the tool bag of the effective communicator. A very commonly used process that has, at its core, the act of giving information, your explanation can be about almost anything. When you explain, you're usually aiming to answer questions such as the why, when and how of events. Your explanation will be a description of an event, process or state of affairs that attempts to illuminate or make clear its causes, context and consequences. Your explanation will use either written or spoken language and three of the more important ways of explaining involve either verbal or written material or presentations. Each of these has its own set of pros and cons and characteristics. You continued your earlier examination (Chapter 2) of the ways we talk to each other by looking at the way we talk on the telephone and in formal meetings. You also saw that written material enables you to put more thought into, revise or rewrite the words that you use while presentations are, potentially, more immediate and impactful when they are prepared, rehearsed and performed in a thorough and thoughtful manner.

INSTANT TIP

Make sure that *you* really understand what you are trying to explain – otherwise you'll never manage to explain it to someone else.

07

Write words or wrong ways?

We all learn to speak before we learn to write and, perhaps because of this, most of us speak more than we write. Despite this, the written word is still important as a way of communicating. This chapter starts by looking at the history of the written word and then explores the nature, structure and content of written communications and how these can be made more effective. Punctuation style and clarity in the written word are explored and the FOG, SMOG and Flesch indices are introduced.

The written word

The written word has been around for some time. Some 6,000 years ago it began its evolutionary journey from pictographs or stylised pictures of real objects and people to the written material that you use today. Recorded on clay tablets, this early form of writing was created and used by an 'elite' of priests and merchants for commercial purposes such as accounts and trading. As time passed it began to be used for other things – recording laws, events, decrees, decisions and sending messages and instructions.

Since that time, both the nature and uses of the written word have continued to change and multiply – as has our access to it. In the fifteenth century, the invention of the hand printing press by Johannes Gutenberg made it possible to print several hundred sheets of text in a day – a considerable improvement on the four sheets per day previously generated by hand copyists. In the early 1800s this quantum leap in the production of printed written material was overtaken, in its turn, by the introduction of the cylinder press with automatic inking. In the twentieth century, the introduction of Xerographic office photocopying and the widespread availability of personal computers continued this process of change. All of this means that we have become able to mass produce written material at rates as high as 40,000 to 60,000 thousand sheets an hour and, using personal computers, electronic or email, fax machines and laser or inkjet printers, to create and transmit text as and when we want. As Marshall McLuhan said: 'Gutenberg made everybody a reader, Xerox made everybody a publisher.'

But, even now – in the early twenty-first century, this river of change continues to flow. For the bandwidth of our written communication has expanded by leaps and bounds. You can now digitally record the material that you write and read; your reports, letters, newspapers and books can be stored on flash drives, memory sticks, hard disks, CDs and DVDs. Technological convergence gives you the opportunity to read this material on the screens of your desk or laptop computers, your electronic notepads, personal digital assistants and your mobile telephones. You can also log on to the internet, using copper cable, optical fibre, wireless or satellite based systems, and gain access to written material on a worldwide basis. As a result, you can now, in your office or your home, download and print written material the original of which is held on the other side of the planet. What all of this means is that we all have access to more and more written material and that these are becoming increasingly based on the electron's spin rather than the complex long chain molecules of cellulose-based paper. This increasing availability of the written word allied with a worldwide upward shift in literacy levels has enabled us all to gain access to sources of information that, historically, have been available only to a privileged few. As a result, our view of the world has irretrievably changed.

Such is the power of the written word.

Written material and spoken words

So how does this written word differ from that other potent way of communicating – the spoken word? For you use both of these and, when you do, they both enable you to communicate facts, feelings, opinions and values. But, as you'll be aware, there are differences between them. One view of these differences tells us that **speech** is:

- dynamic
- ephemeral
- generally, though not always, fixed in time
- often spontaneous
- closely related to and dependent upon:
  - the situation in which it's spoken, and
  - the non-verbal or body language of the speaker and listener(s)
- a two-way process of communication that directly and immediately involves the listener.

Whereas **written material** is:

- rarely, if ever, written and read at the same time
- persistent over time
- able to be re-used and duplicated

- capable of redistribution in new situations, and regarded as proper communication when it is redistributed
- not linked to a context or situation
- often seen as an object
- able to be revised and rewritten before being released as a communication
- often created by a writer working alone and then read by a reader who reads alone
- usually free from the need for rapid, urgent responses
- more constrained by rules and conventions than spoken language, especially as regards form.

What this tells you is that the spoken word and the written word sit in quite different places on the spectrum of ways that you use to communicate. At one end of this spectrum you'll find your formal and prepared written material – such as books or reports, with their rigid, often stylised, form and structured contents. At the other end is your everyday speech with its much looser, far less formal structure and spontaneous nature. Most, but not all, of your written material will lie towards the planned and formal end of this spectrum. However, there is an area where speech and text overlap. There you'll find the informal, unprepared speech and the informal handwritten note which is 'dashed off'.

But formality or planning aren't the only ways in which your written and spoken words differ. For example, written material generally uses more words, more polysyllabic words and fewer personal words or references than speech. This material is also organised differently; it has different rules and regulations about the order and relationship of words (syntax) and the meanings that are allocated to them (semantics). For example, a written text – such as a report – will contain paragraphs, topic sentences and other structural elements. These give you, as a reader, signals or signposts about the structure or logical sequence of the text. Speech, however, rarely has these structural elements.

Spontaneous natural speech will display false starts, changes of direction and will often ignore grammatical rules – rules that generally only apply to the written language.

Nevertheless, despite all these differences, your experience will tell you that the written word can and does make a considerable contribution to your communications.

What and where?

When you think about your exposure to the written word, you'll soon realise that you're exposed to a wide variety of written material. You read, for example, newspapers, magazines, advertisements, books, letters, reports, posters, electronic mail, faxes, text on your television and computer screens, and notices and signs. Most of this material is surprisingly durable and mobile. It can be moved from place to place and can be kept or stored as long as the material on which it is printed survives. In the right form and the right place, written material can literally bypass the centuries and span the continents.

But, despite all of this, the material still only communicates with you in ways that are indirect. The written word lacks the directness of the spoken word; it has less impact, it contains less emotion. But it is, nevertheless, flexible. For the written word can be:

- formal (a typed letter) or informal (an email, mobile phone text or a handwritten note)
- brief (a one-sentence note) or lengthy (a 90,000-word book)
- an expression of an individual style or written formulaically
- written in ways that conform to 'rules' about style and presentation or structured in ways that are original and creative

- easily copied, providing physical evidence of transmission and content, or destroyed after reading
- sent to just one person or a number of people at the same time.

Like the rest of your communications the written word can be used for a variety of purposes. Examples of these include notices (*Stop, Turn Here, etc.*), instructions (*Place part A on top of Part D, etc.*), written advertisements that try to influence you to buy this or that, and the reports and memos of your workplace that provide you with information.

What all of this will tell you is that the potential contribution that written text can make to your workplace communications is considerable. But, in order to make that happen, you are going have to make sure that, when you create your written text, you are clear about:

- who you are writing to
- what the purpose of your text is, and
- in what style you're going to create that text.

So, what you need to do now is look firstly at how you write, and then secondly at how the style and clarity of what you write affects the value of your written words as a way of communicating.

Paper and ink

The act of writing and doing it well is a complex and demanding one. When you write, you draw upon many of your skills and much of your knowledge and experience. You need to know, for example, how to structure sentences, how to plan your use of the time that you have available and how to research the topic of your writing. You also need to know what is 'right', in terms of style and content, for the readers of your material.

The ways that you use to create that written text are often as individual as you are. Some writers take a long time to think about what they are going to write and then commit it to paper or screen in an intense spasm of creativity and in a form that has little need for editing or revision. Others are more systematic in their approach, assembling the final work from increments, each of which is created by steady and consistent labour at the keyboard or writing table. But, however it is done, this process of writing has three key stages: Planning, Creating and Revising.

Planning

Many of the documents, books, letters, reports, notes and memos that you write are planned. This planning can take up as much as half of the total time required for the production of the final text or document. This planning is, of course, about your future actions. It includes, for example, the acts of defining your writing goals – such as 400 words per day, the tasks of preparing and organising your material and activities – such as making sure you've enough cartridges for your inkjet printer, and the work involved in identifying potential content – such as identifying chapter or section content. This planning has four key stages, each of which asks you to make decisions; decisions that will mould your future text. For these stages are about the:

- purpose
- readers
- nature, and
- content of your future text.

The process of creating your text cannot begin until you have made all of these decisions. Get them right and you'll have made a significant contribution to the quality and effectiveness of your final text.

What's the purpose?

The first planning decision that you need to take is about the purpose of your text. Is it, for example, intended to inform or instruct the reader or is it to act as a record of events or decisions? This, the purpose of your text, must be decided and understood before you go any further. Without it your preparation and writing will lack focus and stand little chance of having any real impact on the reader. The best of purposes can be expressed in a single short sentence. For example, the purpose of a letter might be expressed as:

> *To place on record my disagreement with Mr S's actions on 9 December*

or

> *To state my reasons for disagreeing with Mr S on 9 December.*

These are quite different objectives and each will result in a letter that is significantly different to the other. One acts as a record while the other intends to inform and perhaps persuade.

Identifying the purpose of your text is a key step in its generation. For it will affect the style of your writing, the structure of the document and the formality of its text. But even when you've decided the purpose of your text you aren't yet ready to generate it. For now, you must decide who the readers are to be.

Who are the readers?

If your written communications are to be effective then you must, before you write them, be clear about:

- who the reader is
- what he or she already knows

- what interests he or she has
- what he or she wants or needs to know
- what 'jargon' or terminology he or she will understand.

All of these will influence the style and content of your text. For example, a document written to describe the British Government's decision to adopt the European Monetary Unit or Euro will be written in quite different ways when it is written for:

- a House of Commons Select Committee, or
- the readers of a tabloid newspaper.

These groups of readers differ significantly in their interests, vocabularies, levels of knowledge and needs, and all of these will influence the way the document is written. If you're going to be a successful workplace communicator then you have to take a conscious and considered decision about who your intended readers are. Once you've done this, you can start to identify what their particular set of interests and characteristics are – a step that if done well will go a long way towards ensuring that the content and style of the resulting document meets their needs.

Once this decision is taken you'll be ready to move on to the next one.

What's the nature?

You've already decided what the purpose of your text is and who its intended readers are. Both of these exert a significant effect upon the next factor that you have to take a planning decision about – the nature of your text. For example, a document whose purpose is to brief the members of a company board about a hostile takeover bid should be:

- systematic with its contents presented in a logical order
- succinct so that it can be read quickly
- complete so that no important information is omitted
- accurate in that its factual content is correct and verifiable.

A document like this will probably not take more than five sides of A4 paper and possess a limited structure consisting of headings. However, a report that informs company board members about potential candidates for takeover bids will need to be:

- comprehensive so that all potential candidates for takeover and supporting data are given
- accurate in that its factual content is correct and verifiable and that opinions and interpretations are identified
- clear in that its conclusions and recommendations are identified and understandable
- structured in such a way that its contents are presented in an ordered and accessible manner.

A report like this will be large and have several comprehensive appendices containing most of the detailed supporting information. Its structure will reflect the complexity and detail of the subject but will, nevertheless, contain a short summary to enable busy (or lazy) readers to identify its main conclusions.

The decision you take about the nature of your text must also take into account such factors as the time or information available, existing conventions and previous relationships with readers or reader groups. For example, lack of time and a good previous relationship may lead you to write a brief and informal letter to a colleague whereas a bad previous relationship will lead to a formal, detailed and thoughtful letter – whatever time is available.

Having established the purpose, readership and nature of the document, you must now take the final decision of your preparation.

What information?

All of your previous decisions – about the purpose, readership and nature of text – come together to help you when you face this, your final planning decision – a decision about the information that you need.

For example, a limited amount of information is needed when you write a brief and informal note or email to colleagues to remind them that they had promised to provide some data. However, if you need to write a formal report – on sales trends over the past five years – then you'll need a much larger amount of information. Your earlier decisions about the purpose, readership and nature of your text should have given you some pretty broad hints about your document's information needs. However, there's still the potential for you to waste a considerable amount of time and effort collecting and collating irrelevant information. Whatever the size or nature of the document, the process of collecting the necessary information should ensure that:

- only relevant, accurate information is collected, and that
- facts are separated from both opinions and inferences.

Even at this early stage in the writing process it's worthwhile, particularly for the larger documents, to classify the information that you collect – for ease of future use. For shorter documents such as letters, however, that classification may be limited to a few notes about topics or areas that you want to cover in the letter. The larger the document then the greater the need to do this and the more comprehensive the classification. Generating a structured classification of material can also act as an aid to information collection.

Now that you've taken these decisions and completed your planning it's time to move on to the next phase of the process – that of generating your text.

Generating text

The ways in which text is generated are complex and not well understood. At its most basic level, generating text involves the physical actions of forming words by using pen or pencil on a piece of paper or keyboard strokes that show up on a computer screen. To do this effectively you need to be able to manipulate the pen or pencil and press the keys of a keyboard. You also need to be able to structure sentences, spell words and punctuate your text.

But that's not all that's needed.

Your own experience will tell you that you rarely instantly generate perfect and well-rounded phrases and sentences. Your first efforts are often imperfect and you then have to make decisions about when and how to revise that text – without inhibiting or losing the creative thread. One of the theories about how you generate text suggests that it's done in two stages – that of forming an idea and then of converting that idea into words. However, another text generation theory suggests that written text is created as you write rather than being a reproduction of something that you hold in your mind. The speed and effectiveness of your text generation is significantly influenced by how familiar you are with the task of writing. Despite the fact that this act of generating text is complex and only partly understood, it is, nevertheless, one that you embrace on a regular basis.

Revising

Revising is about identifying and implementing changes in your written text. But this revision can take place at any time in the writing process and can involve the re-examination and change of existing plans, goals, methods and, of course, of text. However, most of your revision will focus on the written text. It can be concerned with changing either:

- the meaning of the text, or
- that text's spelling, grammar, structure, etc.

When you revise your text you might:

- add to it, or
- delete from it, or
- substitute new text or words for parts of it, or
- consolidate or extend it.

Experienced writers revise a lot; they often undertake radical changes to the content and form of the text, suppressing any concerns they might have about its detail until its core concepts are right. Writers who use computers find that word processing software with text editing facilities like *'cut'* and *'paste'* help considerably with the process of text revision.

But, however you do it, text revision takes up a limited and minor part of the overall time devoted to the composing process.

Style

The style you use for your writing is important – not only does it reflect your individuality, it also tells your readers how you view them. As such style can exert a considerable influence upon how effective your writing is. You can, for example, write in ways that are:

- formal or informal
- general or particular
- specialised or lay
- complex or simple
- indeterminate or precise
- rational or emotional
- reasoned or exhortative.

When you choose the style that you will adopt to write a particular piece of text you should take into account:

- the expectations and needs of the readers
- your relationship to those readers, and
- the nature of the document.

This means that the Chief Executive Officer (CEO) of a company will adopt a certain style in writing a general letter to all of his or her employees but will use a different style in writing the annual report to the shareholders. Similarly, as a manager, you'll need to choose whether to write a letter in an informal or formal style when reminding team members of the need to observe good time keeping. As an effective workplace communicator you'll need to be sensitive to these issues; you'll need to write in a style that reflects your relationship with your readers, you'll need to think through what the reader might expect from you and you'll need to anticipate the reader's probable reactions to a given style. However, developing your own individual style of writing is a 'must-do' process if you wish to communicate effectively through the medium of the written word.

The point of punctuation

The act of punctuation is often thought of as the application of rules – such as how and when to use commas, apostrophes and colons – when you write. Indeed, the *Oxford English Dictionary* adds weight to this view when it tells us that punctuation is 'the practice, action, or system of inserting points or other small marks into texts'.

But that's not all there is to punctuation. The punctuation marks that you use are signals to your readers – signals that are aimed at helping them to understand what you've written. For example, when you speak you add meaning, emphasis and clarity to what you are saying by pausing, stopping, or changing the tone of your voice. But when you write it's the punctuation marks that you use that should do this. This sort of punctuation is, as *The Times* 'Guide to English Style and Usage' tells you, 'a courtesy to help readers understand a story'.

Here are some hints on how to make sure that your written communications contain that courtesy:

1. Make sure that it's not your writing style – rather than your punctuation – that's getting in the way.
2. Make sure that you know about the rules of punctuation but, more importantly, understand how and when to use them.
3. Remember that the full stop is the best punctuation.

Clear words and readability

The ease with which your readers do, or don't, understand what you write depends upon its clarity and readability. A text may be grammatically perfect, excellently punctuated and contain short, jargon-free sentences and paragraphs – and yet may not be easily read or understood. But the clarity or readability of your texts can be measured and Table 7.1 identifies a number of the measures for readability. The most popular of these methods is the FOG index – invented by Robert Gunning in 1944. Despite its tongue-in-cheek title this index will tell you the American school grade level of reading difficulty of your text. The scale of this index runs from six to 16 and a value of 12 or more is usually taken to indicate that the text may be difficult to read. The Flesch Index is an alternative that is designed for use on adult texts and the Flesch Reading Ease Index scale runs from zero to 100 with increasing ease of readability. 'Standard' writing is described as averaging around 17 words per sentence and 147 syllables per hundred words with a resulting index of 64.

Table 7.1: Readability indices

FOG index

This index gives the US school grade necessary for comprehension of text and is calculated by adding together average number of words per sentence and the percentage of words with more than three syllables, then multiplying the sum by 0.4.

SMOG index

SMOG stands for *Simple Measure of Gobbledegook* and the index is calculated by multiplying the total number of words in a text by 30, dividing the result by the number of sentences, taking the square root of the result and multiplying it by three.

FLESCH index

This is designed for adult texts and is calculated by finding the average number of words per sentence, multiplying that average by 1.015, subtracting the result from 206.8 giving Result 1. Result 2 is calculated by finding the number of syllables per hundred words and multiplying this by 0.846. Subtracting Result 2 from Result 1 gives us the index.

POWER – SUMNER – KEARL index

Designed for primary school tests, this index is calculated by finding the average number of words per sentence and multiplying it by 0.0778, then finding the number of syllables per 100 words and multiplying it by 2.029. The two results are added together to give the PSK index.

STICHT index

This index was designed by the US Army to test functional literacy and is calculated by finding the ratio of single syllable words to total words for the text, multiplying it by 15 and then subtracting the result from 20.

Table 7.2: FOG, SMOG and Flesch Index example

Index example

Before sample

The fact that all organic and inorganic entities and artefacts go through, on this planet at least, cycles of change and decay is a well established and integral feature of life. The level of integration of this fact into human culture is total, encompassing and influencing religion, philosophy, psychiatry, economics and marketing and many other areas of our lives. One numerate view of the failure patterns associated with this cycle of change is shown by the bath-tub curve. Whilst not presuming to be all encompassing this view of failure patterns does coincide with significant areas of experience and evidence for both plant, equipment and human beings.

Totals : Words = 107   Sentences = 4
        Syllables = 187   Words with > three syllables = 11
FOG Index = 14.81 SMOG index = 84.99 Flesch Index = 31.8

After sample

The fact that all organic and inorganic entities and artefacts go through, on this planet at least, cycles of change and decay is a well-known feature of life. This fact also influences many aspects of our lives including religion, philosophy, psychiatry, economics and marketing. One view of the pattern of change and failure is shown by the bath tub curve. Whilst this does not represent all types of failure, it does agree with much of the evidence for both plant, equipment and human beings.

Totals : Words = 85   Sentences = 4
        Syllables = 131   Words with > three syllables = 5
FOG Index = 10.85 SMOG index = 75.75 Flesch Index = 54.85

It should, however, be stressed that these and other indices are not measures of or guides to good writing. They represent measures that can be used to support and refine your judgement about what is the 'right' style for your text. Take a look at Table 7.2 on page 131 for an example of the use of the FOG, SMOG and Flesch indices.

Readability or clarity in your written words can also come about from the way that you use words. At its best, your writing should be simple and direct and use:

- the familiar instead of the far-fetched
- the concrete instead of the abstract
- the short instead of the long.

Summary

In this chapter you saw that the power of the written word is considerable. You also saw that the written texts are generally structured, formal and planned and involve the use of rules about the syntax, semantics and grammar in their generation. The generation of this written text involves the stages of planning, creating and revising. Planning absorbs most of the time taken for this overall process and involves decisions about the text's:

- purpose
- readers
- nature, and
- content.

There are few rules about the creation of text and revising your text will involve the assessment and possible change of its content, structure and meaning.

INSTANT TIP

When you're writing, first make sure that you've really got something to say and then say it as clearly and as succinctly as you can.

08

Are you connected?

The world has changed quite a lot since the invention of first, the internet in 1969, then email in 1971 and then the mobile phone in 1973. While email is still the most popular internet communication tool, other ways of communicating such as email discussion groups, Usenet news, chat groups, video conferencing, VoIP or internet telephony, texting and SMS have blossomed into being and are now in popular use in e-conferences, webinars, social networks, and collaborative content creation. This chapter looks at the how, why, when, drawbacks and benefits of using these and other forms of electronic communication in the workplace.

Faster and further

The technology of the world has changed significantly since the telephone was first invented in 1876. For now, with a telephone no bigger than a small chocolate bar, you can talk to people almost anywhere in the world and tap into the databanks of huge computers on the other side of the planet. But that's not all that's changed. For, since the first laboratory-based electronic computers using binary code ran in the 1940s, computers have continued to evolve and change. As a result you now have, on your desk or in your lap, a computer that is one of over a billion estimated to be in use worldwide. Using chips with very large scale integrated (VLSI) circuits, your computer runs software that provides you with access to word processing, spreadsheets, databases, games, and numerous personal productivity and special-purpose software systems. It also gives you access to the internet, allowing you to email people almost everywhere and to gain entry to the World Wide Web with its treasure troves of information and resources.

But why, you might ask, has all this happened and why has it happened so fast?

The answer is, of course, a simple and obvious one – it's because we all, as the human race, want and need to communicate with each other. In the rest of this chapter you'll look at some of the ways in which technology can help you do that.

The internet

There will always be arguments about the when and where of the birth of the internet. Nevertheless, what history does tell us is that the first message ever to be sent over a network of linked computers was transmitted over the Advanced Research Projects Agency Network (ARPANET) in San Francisco at 10.30 p.m. on 29 October 1969. This network – developed by the United States Department of Defense – inspired the creation, in 1978, of a British, American, Canadian and French collaborative international packet-switched network service that had grown, by 1981, out from Europe and America to include Canada, Hong Kong and Australia. However, the internet, or World Wide Web as you now know it, didn't really come into existence until 30 April 1993, when the Geneva-based Conseil Européen pour la Recherche Nucléaire (CERN) announced that the World Wide Web would be available for free use by anyone. This World Wide Web had been invented by Sir Tim Berners-Lee in 1989 and then further developed until, by late 1990, the basic building blocks of the internet – a web browser, web server, and web pages – were available.

Since then, the World Wide Web hasn't stopped growing and changing.

Now it's estimated that more than one in five people in the world use the internet – a usage rate that mushroomed by around 300 per cent between 2000 and 2008. But that's not the only thing that's grown on the internet. The worldwide internet service provider Yahoo! now provides a search interface in at least 38 international markets and a number of languages and the most used search engine on the web – Google – uses an estimated 450,000 servers in 25 locations throughout the world.

All of this has happened because the internet:

- is based on an open or non-proprietary standard for transmitting data from one computer to another
- is transparent and public, and
- is easy to use.

But these aren't the only reasons for the internet's growth. For the internet is, above all, an easy way for people to communicate with each other. There are a considerable number of ways in which that happens. These include email, email discussion groups, Usenet news, chat groups, video and audio conferencing, blogs, VoIP, e-conferencing/data conferencing, web conferencing, webinars, wikis (see later in this chapter), and 'social' websites such as Twitter, Facebook, MySpace, YouTube, AOL, Slashdot and virtual worlds such as Second Life.

What you'll do now is to take a look at the more significant of these and the ways in which they can enhance your workplace communications.

Email

Electronic mail was in use before the invention of email as we now know it. In its earliest form it was used to leave notes in another user's file directory when both of you used the same computer. Once computer networks appeared things had to change – these messages needed an 'envelope' and an 'address'. In 1971 Ray Tomlinson changed things by using the @ symbol to give messages an address, such as

HarryScoble@HarryScoble's computer

That system remains in use to this day.

Email is the internet's most important application and its most widely used facility with over 100 billion email messages being sent daily. The reasons for this popularity include the fact that email:

- is easy to use
- is cheap
- doesn't need your computer to be switched on when somebody emails you
- can easily carry attachments – such a picture, an article, or a piece of music
- can be answered as and when you want
- can be sent to one person or thousands of people.

Another reason for the popularity of email is that its structure is simple and straightforward. For each email has:

- a header – that contains information such as message summary and the ID code or name of the sender and receiver
- a body – that contains the message, sometimes with a signature block at the end.

Your email's header tells you:

- who it's from: email address, and/or name of the sender
- who it is going to: email address(es) and/or name(s) of the message's recipient(s)
- what the message's subject is: very brief, single line summary of the message contents
- when the message was sent: local time and date
- who has been sent copies: Cc: carbon copy, Bcc: Blind or hidden carbon copy
- who to reply to: email address that should be used to reply to the sender
- In-Reply-To: ID of message that this is a reply to.

Table 8.1 on the following page contains a list of email 'etiquette' points that should help you to make your emailing more effective.

However, the high volume of email on the internet isn't just due to email's simplicity and ease of use. For many of the emails that are sent each day consist of what is called 'spam'. Spam is the name that's given to unsolicited bulk commercial email. We all get it. It's frustrating, confusing and annoying; most of it is sent by fewer than 200 'spammers' and, worldwide, it costs billion of dollars in terms of lost productivity and IT system operating costs. One FTSE firm recently estimated that dealing with pointless emails cost it £39 million a year. Recent research indicates that the chances of you finding spam when you open your email inbox increases when you start your email address with the letters A, M, S, R, P or U. But spam isn't just frustrating. For it can also contain an attack on the security of the personal data that you hold in your computer (phishing) or aim to take over complete control of your computer so that it becomes what's called a 'zombie' personal computer: one that, as part of a network of similar computers or a 'botnet', can be used by other people to send spam out over the internet.

Table 8.1: Email etiquette points

When you email:
DO:

- be concise and to the point
- avoid long sentences and words like 'urgent' or 'important' unless your email really is important or urgent
- make sure that your email has a subject heading
- use proper spelling, grammar and punctuation
- try to answer quickly
- read through your email *before* you send it
- use subject words or phrases that:
  - are concise and meaningful, and
  - tell the reader what your email is really about
- use cc: or bcc: fields sparingly
- keep your language gender neutral.

DON'T:

- write in CAPITALS (this gives the impression of shouting)
- use email to discuss confidential or personal information
- open spam – delete it unopened
- attach files unnecessarily
- use 'Reply to All' unless it's appropriate
- use abbreviations and emoticons (e.g. a smiley face)
- ever send or forward emails containing material that is libellous, defamatory, offensive, racist or obscene
- forward virus hoaxes and chain letters.

Filters based on email word content or Bayesian filtering can reduce, but never eliminate, the flood of spam into your inbox.

Nevertheless, despite all these problems, email does give you a quick and easy way of communicating – provided you use it well.

Internet forums

An internet forum uses a software suite that will enable you to hold discussions with other people via email, the content of which can be posted for general access. Forums like this are also commonly referred to as web forums, newsgroups (as in Usenet), message boards, discussion boards, electronic discussion groups, discussion forums or bulletin boards. Popular themes for these forums include technology, computer games, video games, sports, fashion, religion and politics. Regular forum users are said to develop a sense of community. The messages posted are displayed in chronological order or as threaded discussions. You'll find that some forums allow anonymous contribution while others will require you to register as a user. Contributions to forums like this are usually monitored by forum administrators/moderators. These administrators usually have the authority to edit or delete your contributions, close the board and even ban you as a member. Using a forum like this will enable you and your co-workers to communicate at a distance and do so in ways that can also be seen and accessed by a larger community – such as a department or research group. Forum software packages are widely available on the internet. They can also be integrated into existing websites or blogs to allow visitors to post comments on articles.

One version of this way of communicating via the internet is run by the international coffee chain, Starbucks. A website – called 'My Starbucks Idea' – acts as an open forum for customer ideas about how the 'Starbucks experience' could be improved. These are then read and evaluated by 'Idea Partners' – Starbucks' employees who are experts in their respective fields – who then take a combination of the most popular and most innovative ideas that are the best fit for Starbucks and present them to key decision-makers within the company. Examples of ideas adopted include a 'bring-your-own mug' discount and offering school teachers a complimentary cup of brewed coffee on Mondays during the month of September.

Blogs

A blog (or web log) is an internet website that contains regular entries – such as commentary, descriptions of events, graphics or video – rather like a diary. These entries are usually displayed in reverse chronological order and readers are often encouraged to leave comments. Blogs are usually, but not always, created by individuals and, as such, can be idiosyncratic or based on a minority viewpoint. Nevertheless, there are, at the moment, over 100 million blogs on the internet. Free and open source software for blog creation is readily available on the internet but before you rush off to create your own blog, a word of warning! Several bloggers have been sacked for allegedly bringing their employers into disrepute by writing a blog describing their everyday working life.

Apart from the personal blogs mentioned above, there are also:

- **Microblogs** – such as 'Twitter', which limits an entry to 140 characters – called a 'tweet' – and seeks to capture a 'moment in time' (see Figure 8.1). Microblogs like this are used by not only individuals but also by corporations such as Cisco Systems, Whole Foods Market, Dell, Zappos.com, Comcast, Los Angeles Fire Department, NASA, news outlets such as CNN and the BBC and several 2008 US presidential candidates.
- **Corporate blogs** – used either to enhance internal communication in an organisation or externally for marketing, branding or public relations purposes.

- **Device based blogs** – defined by which type of device is used to compose the blog, as in a 'moblog' that's written on a mobile phone or PDA.
- **Subject based blogs** – these include political blogs, travel blogs, house blogs, fashion blogs, project blogs, education blogs, classical music blogs, quiz blogs, legal blogs and blogs on many other subjects or genres.
- **Question and answer blogs** – these answer questions submitted either via a submittal in the form of an email, or telephone or VoIP (see later in chapter) call.

Figure 8.1: Twittering history

Twit sent by Barack Obama at 11.34am, 5 November 2008:

We just made history. All of this happened because you gave your time, talent and passion. All of this happened because of you. Thanks

Barack Obama

Podcasting

Podcasting is an interesting and developing form of blog. Initially known as 'audio-blogging', the word 'podcast' grew from a combination of the words 'iPod' and 'broadcast' – the Apple iPod being the portable media player for which the first podcasting scripts were developed. Using audio files – instead of text – to reach its audience, podcasting's range and content has grown from a few radio-style shows generated by individuals to a huge range of other uses. The Apple iTunes online store, for example, currently offers access to over 100,000 podcast episodes and video podcasts are also available.

The span of the subject matter covered by these podcasts is considerable. It ranges from the individual and idiosyncratic – as in those generated by independent creators, such as Adam Curry and Stephen Fry – to the more commercial podcasts assembled by big corporate names – such as, for example, the BBC, Home Box Office, National Public Radio, Canadian Broadcasting Corporation, *The New York Times*, *Financial Times*, Starbucks, Greenpeace, Ford, London Business School, Heineken, General Motors and Royal British Legion.

The technology involved in creating and 'broadcasting' a podcast isn't difficult. If you're going to podcast you'll need software such Audacity, LAME, iTunes or Windows Media Player and SmartFTP – all of which are free to download and use. You'll also need some audio equipment – such as a microphone – and have carefully thought through the what, why and how of your podcast before you start. Once you've created your podcast you can use it to proselytise your individual views or interests, or sell your company's products and services.

Wikis

'Wiki' is said to be the Hawaiian word for 'fast' and wikis are collections of web pages that have been created in such a way that anyone who accesses them can contribute to or modify their content. As such, a wiki operates in ways that:

- invite you, as a user, to edit any page or to create new pages
- seek to involve you in an ongoing process of creation and collaboration that results in a website that's constantly changing
- ensure that pages are collaboratively written.

The collaborative encyclopedia, Wikipedia, is probably the best-known wiki but you can also use them in the workplace to provide intranets and knowledge management systems. Despite the fact that wikis can be edited by almost anybody and hence run the risk of degrading into the internet equivalent of graffiti, they do seem to work very well.

Social networking sites

These sorts of website aim to build online communities of people who either share interests and activities or want to explore other people's interests and activities. Users connect and interact with each other in a variety of ways – such as email and instant messaging.

Sites like these are being used by millions of people on a regular, hour-by-hour basis. They can be based on a variety of things – such as being former classmates or the need for a way of keeping in touch with friends. MySpace (118 million users in more than 29 countries) and Facebook (135 million users, over 60 languages) appear to be the most widely used but others – such as Bebo, Skyrock Blog, Orkut , Friendster and Cyworld – are also popular.

These sites reflect the fact that social networking has always been important – even before the internet. But with these sorts of sites people can now network globally and, in so doing, keep in touch and test ideas with friends and acquaintances across the planet. Recent research indicates that communication on these software-enabled networks is more like texting rather than emailing and that communication takes place in exchanges that can extend over days – without any perceived pressure to respond. In the world of work, networks like these enable people based either in different parts of the world, different departments, or even on different floors of a building, to quickly communicate, and share knowledge and information with friends and colleagues everywhere. British

Telecom, for example, uses an internal, social software-based network so that people of different disciplines – who aren't necessarily in the some location – can collaborate, bringing their combined knowledge, experience and expertise to bear on the tasks and problems that the organisation faces.

More recently many social networking sites have made it easy for users to link to other services such as video hosting sites. Some even enable users to build video into their messages and pages, so building on other networks and interests and increasing the potential linkages. These social networks aim, like email, to connect people at low cost and as such they are used by businesses to:

- act as a customer relationship management tool
- advertise
- keep in touch with contacts around the world.

Current examples of business social networking websites are LinkedIn.com – a site that aims to connect professionals and claims to have more than 25 million registered users from 150 different industries, and Xing – a site that claims to have 6.5 million users and is available in 16 languages, including Mandarin.

But these aren't the only sort of social network websites. IBM currently implements a social network within its W3 intranet. Currently, around 85 per cent of IBM's 380,000 employees are said to use this intranet and the aim of this social network – called Beehive – is to encourage employees to establish social and professional connections and so to build networks. Other social websites are targeted at using the power of the social networking model for social good. Current examples of these include SixDegrees.org and Network for Good. Both of these sites encourage the use of the Charity Badge – a widget to be used on websites, blogs, social networks or email for the promotion of a humanitarian cause or charity project.

Virtual worlds

A virtual world is a computer-based simulated environment that its users can inhabit and interact with via a two- or three-dimensional graphical representation or avatar (an alter ego). These modelled worlds may be similar in appearance to the real world or depict fantasy worlds and their 'rules' – such as gravity, communication, topography, etc. – may, or may not, be based on the real world. Current examples include Active Worlds, Club Penguin, Google Lively, Roma Victor and Second Life.

But these aren't just websites where you play a game. In Second Life, for example, a number of educational institutions – such as Sussex University and the Open University – are running virtual classrooms and discussion sections. Business also makes its presence felt and many companies and organisations have set up a presence, in one form or another, in Second Life. Among the organisations that have done this are 20th Century Fox, ABN AMRO Bank, Adidas Reebok, American Apparel, American Cancer Society, Axel Springer AG, BBC Radio 1, British Telecom, Cisco, Dell, Disney, Harvard Law School and Harvard Extension School, ING Group, Mazda, MTV, National Physical Laboratory (UK), PA Consulting Group, Reuters, Sky News, Starwood Hotels, Sun Microsystems, Telecom Italia, Toyota, Universal Motown Records Group, University of Southern California's Center on Public Diplomacy and Wells Fargo. British Telecom, for example, has its own 'private island' within Second Life where avatars can make calls via a red payphone, send text messages, run a teleconference and even order a pizza to be delivered to their real world address.

By using these virtual worlds, companies gain the chance to test customer reaction and receive feedback on new or potential products.

VoIP

VoIP is an acronym that stands for Voice over Internet Protocol. This is a bundle of software and sometimes hardware that enables people to use the internet to make telephone calls. One advantage of VoIP is that these telephone calls don't involve any charge – providing the receiver has the same software – beyond the usual internet access charge.

The most popular VoIP systems are Skype and Vonage. Apart from the usual free computer-to-computer calls, Skype also allows you (at a cost) to receive calls dialled by regular phone subscribers and to use Skype on your mobile phone. Vonage requires you to become a subscriber and to buy a Vonage branded VoIP router or a phone adapter that connects to your main router or broadband modem. You can then choose your own Vonage telephone number and area code. This can be anywhere in the country of the service regardless of where you actually live. Neither of these services offers access to emergency numbers such as 999. However, their potential benefits for low cost telephone business communications are obvious.

Video conferencing

Video conferencing uses the transmission of audio and video information over the internet to bring people at different sites together for a meeting. This can be a simple point-to-point conference between two locations or a multi-point conference involving people at several locations. Besides transmitting voices and pictures, video conferencing can also be used to share documents, computer-displayed information and whiteboards.

In the workplace, it's argued that video conferencing saves time and money by enabling you and others in distant locations to have meetings at short notice. Technology such as VoIP can also be used together with desktop video conferencing to enable low-cost face-to-face business meetings to take place without leaving your desk. It's also useful when keeping in touch with people who work from home. Video conferencing is now being introduced on a number of online networking websites.

Viral marketing

Viral marketing is an advertising technique that makes use of the networks that exist between people to generate increasing brand awareness or increasing product sales. It does that by encouraging people to voluntarily pass along a marketing message that might be in the form of a video clip, an interactive Flash game, an e-book, an image or even a text message. However, in its basic form, viral marketing doesn't last forever and, after a while, your viral marketing message will degrade and disappear.

However, while it lasts, viral marketing can be effective and successful and notable examples have included those generated by Burger King, TiVo and Cadbury, and the launches of several social websites such as Facebook, YouTube, MySpace and Digg.

Web conferencing (including webinars and webcasts)

Web conferencing is a way of conducting live meetings over the internet. During a web conference each person involved sits at his or her own computer and is connected to other participants via the internet. In order to achieve this you will need to use either an application that has been downloaded on each computer or a web-based application where each person will simply enter a given website address to join the conference. Conferences like this can be quite sophisticated, using slide presentations, live video, VoIP, access to other websites, conference recording for viewing later on another website, use of whiteboards, text 'chat' for live question and answer sessions, polls/surveys, and screen sharing where participants can view anything the presenter currently has on their screen. Web conferencing is often sold as a service and as such hosted on a web server controlled by the service provider.

When a web conference involves a lecture, workshop or seminar then it's often called a webinar or web seminar. Like web conferences, these are interactive with the ability to give, receive and discuss information. These and web conferences contrast with webcasts, in which the data transmission is one way and does not allow interaction between the presenter and the audience. These webcasts use the internet to broadcast live or delayed audio and/or video transmissions such as online courses, lectures or press conferences.

Instant messaging

Instant messaging (IM) gives you the opportunity to have real-time text 'conversations' with one or more other people. It uses the internet or an internal computer network/intranet and is different to email in that it happens in real-time – 'before your eyes' as it were. However, some systems do allow offline messages to be sent.

IM allows effective and efficient communication and as such is being increasingly used in the workplace. IM is used for:

- asking and getting answers to quick, short questions
- co-ordinating what people do
- scheduling tasks
- arranging quick 'get-togethers' or impromptu meetings.

Mobile phones and texting

The first mobile or cell phone call is said to have been made by Dr Martin Cooper in New York on 3 April 1973 and the first commercial mobile phone service was launched in Japan in 1978. From then on things really started to happen and by the end of the first decade of the twenty-first century the number of mobile phone service subscriptions will have passed 3.3 billion, or half of the human population. Now, the numbers of mobile phone subscriptions have exceeded population levels in more than 50 countries. The mobile or cell phone is truly the widest spread technology and the most used gadget on the planet.

But why is this so?

One view will tell you about the changes and benefits brought by the mobile phone to the 'Four Ms' of our lives. For they have changed or contributed to your:

- movement or mobility – you can use them almost anywhere
- moments or use of time – you can use them when you want to
- 'me-ness' – as in it's my phone, my ringtone, etc.
- money – as in I can use it to buy goods and services or check my bank account.

But that isn't all that they bring with them. Now, mobile phones provide, in addition to the standard voice service, a wide range of other services such as short message service (SMS) for text messaging, email, internet access, gaming, Bluetooth (see later in this chapter) and infrared connectivity, a still camera/video recorder together with a multimedia messaging service (MMS) for sending and receiving photos and video.

Sending messages of 160 characters or less and available on most mobile phones, texting is most commonly used in person-to-person messaging, but can also be used to order products and services for mobile phones, or participate in contests. It is extraordinarily popular with over 1.2 million text messages being sent each week in the UK alone. It's not surprising, therefore, to find that it has also developed its own language, some of which – such as FYI or for your information – has crept into common language usage.

In the workplace, texting has been used by political parties – as a much easier, cheaper way of getting to the voters – and by businesses – as when confirming deliveries of goods and services or in providing instant communication between a service provider and a client.

Blue-jacking and Blue-casting

Blue-jacking and Blue-casting have the same root – the sending of unsolicited wireless messages to mobile phones, personal digital assistants (pdas) or laptop computers. Bluetooth is a wireless protocol that uses short-range communications technology to enable data transmission over short distances from fixed and/or mobile devices. Named after a tenth-century king of Denmark, Harald Bluetooth, who was known for his unification of previously warring tribes, Bluetooth enables a wide range of equipment to 'talk' to each other. However, due to its low power, the messages sent have a very limited range – 10 metres or less for mobile phones and pdas and up to 100 metres for laptops.

Blue-jacking, in its most basic form, is rather like email spam. It involves using your mobile phone to send an unsolicited message – such as 'Hello, you've been blue-jacked' – to other Bluetooth enabled phones. Usually harmless, blue-jacking has been used in what are called 'guerrilla' marketing campaigns.

Blue-casting, however, is a much more serious and commercial activity. It involves using a small static server to send messages over Bluetooth to mobile phones, pdas and laptops that have this facility switched on. This server is usually housed in a kiosk or booth in a public place – such as a shopping centre, coffee shop, train station, airport lounge or conference centre. Blue-casting has been used, among other things, to launch a new LandRover, advertise a tennis event, provide music downloads, launch a new iPod in China, advertise BBC TV programmes in train stations and deliver update podcasts at conferences. The technology involved is complex and usually requires the use of experienced consultants.

Online advertising

The first banner advertisement was shown on the internet in 1994 and since then online advertising or advertising of goods and services on the internet has shown considerable growth. Currently, UK advertisers spend more money on online advertising than they do on advertising in newspapers and, in the first quarter of 2007, American advertisers spent some $4.9 billion on online advertising. All of this has happened because, once people get broadband internet connections, they tend to spend more time on the internet and less time reading newspapers and magazines or watching TV and listening to the radio. As a result, advertising has gone online.

But that's not all that's changed. For online advertising has created a new vocabulary that reflects its power and sophistication as you can see below:

- Banner advert: a website graphical advertisement that people click on to reach another advertiser's site.
- Behavourial adverts: these are presented as a response to a surfer's recent online web surfing.
- Clickthrough rates (CTR): the percentage of times that an advert results in the viewer clicking on it.

- Cost per action (CPA): an advertiser only pays for this sort of advert when someone completes a transaction.
- Cost per thousand (CPT): what an advert costs to reach a thousand online viewers.
- Pay-per-click (PPC) advert: the advertiser only pays for this sort of advert when a viewer clicks on it.

All of this reflects the prodigious growth of the internet as a medium of commerce together with the ability that advertisers now have to target consumer groups. It's also part of the price that we have to pay for being able to use the internet. However, if you're responsible for advertising your organisation's products or services you'd do well to consider using it.

What's next – Web 2.0?

If we've learnt anything about the internet since it came into being in 1989 it's that things don't stay still for long. There are always exciting new applications, brand new sites and revisions or upgrades of existing applications and operating systems appearing. Some of these extend our ability to use the internet and become part of our desktop or laptop portfolio of favourites. Others, however, don't achieve this status and drift into some remote and unsupported internet backwater of 'has-beens'.

The pace and nature of these changes is such that, from time to time, it's suggested that the internet itself has moved into a new and different 'state of being'. The latest of these is encapsulated in the term 'Web 2.0'. First used in a 2004 computer conference group discussion, this term, initially, was an attempt to capture the increasing importance of the internet and the growing pace of development of applications/services. Many of these – such as blogs, social networking and podcasting – have been mentioned in this chapter. However, current views of Web 2.0 recognise that these changes are solidly rooted in the original 'Web 1.0' technology and, as such, are logical developments of that technology – rather than a quantum leap into a new paradigm.

Nevertheless, it is worth noting that many of the applications and services created have resulted in a web that is more 'socially connected'; a web in which people can more easily communicate with each other. Whilst this trend is a logical and obvious extension of the original intention of Sir Tim Berners-Lee, the Web's inventor, to create a space that is interactive and all about connecting people, it's also a significant signpost to the ways in which the internet of the future will contribute to your workplace communication.

Summary

In this chapter you've looked at a wide range of the ways in which you can use technology to communicate. Starting with the internet, these included email, internet forums, blogs, podcasting, wikis, social networking sites, virtual worlds, VoIP, video conferencing, viral marketing, web conferencing including webinars and webcasts, instant messaging, mobile phones and texting, blue-jacking and blue-casting, and online advertising.

INSTANT TIP

Always check what's in your email and who you are sending and copying it to – *before you send it*!

09

Does your team talk?

Team is a word that gets used (and misused) quite a lot in the workplace. But real teams – the ones that produce results – are rare animals that take time to grow and develop. Effective communication is key to that process. This chapter looks at the ways and means of the effective team communication – a process that's essential both within the team itself and the environment that the team operates in.

Crowds, groups and teams

People come together quite often and when they do that you'll probably use words like 'crowd', 'committee', 'department, 'group' or 'team' to describe the result. These assemblies of people have enormous variety in both their nature and their purpose. They can, for example, spring into existence because people want to watch or play a sports game, or catch a train or an aeroplane, or protest about something, or even just work together. The places where they happen or function are just as various. They include, for example, factories, offices, assembly plants, theatres, concert halls, cricket grounds, baseball stadiums and football grounds.

But all of this doesn't really tell you very much about these gatherings. For if you're going to understand them and, in particular, understand more about workplace teams, you're going to have to find the answers to questions like:

- how many people are involved?
- how often do they come together?
- are they temporary – or permanent – gatherings?
- what do they want to achieve?
- have these people come together voluntarily – or not?

You'll begin to find some answers when you take your first step towards understanding the team – by looking at two far more common sorts of gathering – the crowd and the group.

The crowd

Being in a crowd is a very common experience – it happens to all of us all of the time and almost everywhere. If you could helicopter up above a crowd what you'd see is a lot of people moving about in ways that are apparently disorganised and random. But if you think about what's happening in a crowd – say, at rush hour in a big city mainline railway station – you'll soon realise that isn't so. For while this crowd appears disorganised, the people in it will actually have a purpose in common. Most of the people in a railway station crowd like this will want to get on a train. But this objective hasn't been discussed, debated, shared or agreed. However, when you look at the objectives of individual crowd members, you'll soon start to see differences. For example, some crowd members will want to get on to one particular train while others will want to get on to another train. Some people won't want to get on a train at all – they'll be meeting someone who has come into the station on a train. These detailed personal objectives can clash with each other – as often happens at rush hour in conflicts over space or seating, or who stands on which part of the platform while waiting for the train to arrive. What this tells you is that when you're in a crowd you rarely act in ways that require other than minimal and basic co-operation with the people around you. This, as you'll soon see, is different to the sorts of things that happen in a group.

Groups

When you start to think about the differences between crowds and groups you'll soon see that some of these are significant. You'll find, for example, that while crowds generally consist of a large, almost unlimited, number of people, groups are smaller and limited in size – usually because group members voluntarily limit the size of the group. You'll also see that while crowd members only have an objective in common and only co-operate at a minimal and basic level, group members generally have a shared objective and act together towards achieving it.

What this and your own experience will tell you is that people in a group:

- share at least one and sometimes several interconnected objectives, and
- do things together to achieve those objectives.

This act of doing things together is important, as you'll see later when you look at teams. It's also one of the reasons why groups get used a lot in our workplaces. But when this happens they aren't always called a 'group'. Other words and titles, such as 'committee', 'council', 'board', 'crew', 'party' or even – though misguidedly – 'team', are often used.

There are two significant factors that influence the way these groups function in the workplace. These are:

- the size of the group, and
- its level of formality or informality.

For example, if you are in a small group, you'll:

- have lots of face-to-face contact with other group members
- share and co-operate quite a lot with those people, and
- exert direct influence on each other, usually about the interests, ideas, standards and beliefs that you have.

But in larger groups – such as the departments and divisions of the organisations that you work in – you'll:

- have less and limited face-to-face contact
- experience restricted sharing and co-operation, and
- only exert indirect influence on each other and then only about 'broad brush' generalised issues or objectives.

When you look at the differences between formal and informal groups you'll find that formal groups, whether large or small:

- are controlled and supervised by a leader
- have goals that are set by the parent organisation
- have communication patterns that flow down from the top
- are usually permanent but can be temporary
- are often subject to changes in membership
- often use competition and rivalry between group members to achieve their ends
- are a well-proven and conventional way of getting things done.

Examples of formal groups include departments, committees, work groups and project control or co-ordination groups. Their purposes, composition and structures are usually spelt out in a formal document and the person appointed to lead the group – its leader or co-ordinator – is responsible for the group's performance. You'll only become a member of this sort of group if you can make a contribution – by virtue of your functional skills or abilities – towards reaching its goals.

Informal groups, however, exist everywhere and come together for quite different reasons and in different ways. These groups:

- spring into being because you and others – rather than the organisation – want them to answer your social needs
- will only continue to exist as long as they answer those needs
- have little or no structure and no need for defined formal roles
- often act as informal communication networks or 'grapevines', and
- exist either within larger formal groups or on their own.

Your membership of an informal group is usually based on friendship or common need – rather than on what you can do.

But among these groups – formal or informal – there also exists a rather unusual and special sort of group – one that's called the team.

Team or group?

Teams – real teams that is – are special. They are also different to almost all the sorts of groups or crowds that you'll generally come across. For this rather unusual and special sort of group – the team – has a special talent. It has the potential to synergise the individual efforts of members into a new whole that is greater than their sum. In an ordinary group, two plus two sometimes equals four, while in a special group or team – and particularly in a good one – that two plus two adds up to five – or more!

But that's not all that's different in a team. For it has:

- a facilitator/coach/co-ordinator rather than a leader
- goals that are set by its members rather than the parent organisation
- communication patterns that flow up *and* down, and
- members that:
  - make decisions together
  - work together co-operatively
  - are jointly responsible for outcomes.

By now, you've probably guessed two things – firstly, that a real team is an usual and rare event and, secondly, that a real team has the potential to make a significant difference to the performance of your workplace. It has that potential because all of its members have one thing in common – the willingness and ability to communicate. When that happens – and keeps on happening – what you get is a team, a team that consists of people who:

- work well together
- do that in ways that combine their individual skills and abilities
- share responsibility for what the team does and what happens in it
- do all of that in order to achieve an outcome that they jointly see to be meaningful.

What do teams do?

Teams like this do all sorts of things. Here are some examples:

Executive teams

These are the teams that run things. They exist at all levels in an organisation and can be in charge of and responsible for groups of co-workers that range in size from hundreds to tens of thousands. In large complex organisations, teams like this report to a Chief Executive Officer (CEO) and monitor and control key aspects of that organisation's performance. Their work is ongoing and continuous.

Front line teams

These are the teams that make or do things. They are, typically, responsible for the functional parts of an organisation such as sales, operations, manufacturing or research. Their work is also ongoing and continuous and they usually report to an executive team. They are responsible for and in charge of the fine detail of how a department or function operates.

Project teams

These teams are in charge of one-shot events or projects. These can be about creating a new factory, auditing the safety levels in an existing factory or examining the causes of an accident. They are often given names like task force, project group or audit team. Their work is not ongoing or continuous but has a fixed remit and a predetermined completion date.

So, now that you know how versatile the team can be, let's take a look at how you can begin to make the shift from being a group to being a productive, effective team.

First steps

The first thing that you need to realise about real teams is that they don't just 'happen'. You are going to have to work hard to create, maintain and sustain a real team – a team that gets results. Teams like this are good to have about and, as a consequence, quite a lot of time has been spent trying to find out how such teams develop and keep their 'cutting edge'. What these studies say is that this happens when the team's members are:

- really good at communicating with each other
- loyal to each other and the team
- able to identify and agree a collective outcome
- keen to co-operate and collaborate in order to achieve that collective outcome
- focused towards creating team – rather than individual – outcomes, and
- able to define these outcomes in ways that are specific, tangible, measurable and meaningful to all team members.

By now you'll have realised that teams like this are very different to the groups of your workplace. But these teams aren't created overnight. If your team is going to function effectively it will need support and understanding from its parent organisation, time to grow and develop, a high degree of autonomy and confidence that its success will be both recognised and rewarded. But that isn't all that your team will need. For it will also need to:

- be the 'right' size
- have the 'right' mix of people in it, and, last but not least
- have an 'environment' that encourages effective communication.

Let's look at each of these in turn.

How many?

Size is important when it comes to teams. Too big a team will mean that your team communications won't be good. As a result, the decisions that get made and problem solutions that get identified won't tap into, or make use of, the skills and knowledge of all the team members. Too small a team and your team communications will be much better but you'll probably find your team is short on skills, expertise and people-time.

So what is the 'right' number?

The pragmatic answer is that the 'right' team size lies within a range of sizes and is influenced by factors such as the demands of the team task, the availability of the 'right' people and the sort of organisation that you're working in.

Here are some simple guidelines that should help you:

- **maximum size**: don't have more than ten people
- **optimum size**: between six and eight people.

However, getting your team size right isn't the only important factor. You also have to make sure that you have the right mix of people.

Who – and why?

The job of selecting the 'right people' for your team is important. Get it wrong and you'll have conflicts, difficulties and a poor team performance; get it right and you'll still have conflicts and difficulties but, in the end, you'll also have a team that works.

Unfortunately the news – that teams need to be carefully selected – hasn't reached everywhere. Many organisations select their teams using the criterion of functional skill alone – ignoring the people skills and personalities of the individuals behind those functional skills. In other situations people get chosen for teams because they are easy to get on with, do what they are told, don't rock the boat, etc. All of this ignores the fact that if you're going to create a team that works then you're going to need people that have:

- the required functional skills, *plus*
- the ability to communicate effectively, *plus*
- 'team' skills.

This means that they will need to have demonstrated their ability to work co-operatively with others and be willing to give up part of their own 'ego-space' in order to become integrated into the team. Getting integrated as a team is not an easy task. One way of bypassing or overcoming the problems involved is to pick people as team members because they have all the above skills plus an ability to carry out at least one of the roles that a balanced team needs. These roles are generally about things like coming up with new ideas, defusing conflict or tension, looking after the team chores, analysing what's happening or even challenging the position of the rest of the team. Research tells us that all 'good' teams have all these roles and, as a result, can operate in ways that are independent of individual efforts or skills.

Finding out whether potential team members are up to these sorts of roles isn't the easiest of tasks. Nevertheless, there is a surprising amount of information about. You can find out, for example, how they've performed in other teams, what their attitudes and responses have been to relevant training and development programmes or what their current or ex-bosses think about their team skills. You can also use one of the commercial team role assessment questionnaires that are available – such as the Belbin Team Roles, MTR–i™ and Margerison–McCann questionnaires.

Table 9.1 shows the description that the Belbin Team Roles selection process gives to the sorts of roles that you will need in your team. You can also use these team member selection systems to help you choose new members of the team when people leave or move on.

Once you've got the right mixture of complementary skills, abilities and experience, your team will have a potential that exceeds, by orders of magnitude, the sum of the abilities and skills of its individual members.

Table 9.1: Belbin Team Roles

Chairperson – described as being 'calm, self-confident and self-controlled', this role clarifies group objectives and sets agendas.

Company Worker – a hard-working practical organiser who turns other team members' ideas into manageable tasks.

Shaper – 'outgoing and dynamic', this role is the task leader, uniting ideas and shaping the application of team effort.

Plant – 'individualistic and unorthodox', this role is the ideas generator for the team but can be detached from practicality.

Resource Investigator – often described as the fixer of the team this role has high communication skills and social acceptability.

Monitor–Evaluator – the analyst of the team who tends to be 'sober, unemotional and prudent'.

Team Worker – 'mild and sensitive', this role listens and communicates well and often smoothes conflict.

Completer–Finisher – a perfectionist who has to check every detail.

Effective team communication

Once your team is selected then it's time for the potential that's contained in this motley crew of individuals to be turned into actual, demonstrable performance. The key to doing this lies in the way that your team communicates.

Creating a team culture that encourages effective communication is a process that starts at the first team meeting. For it's there that the process begins, by which this collection of individuals will evolve, change and develop into an effective, working, results-generating team. It may also be the first time that the team comes together and it's a meeting that has the primary purpose of generating the Team Charter.

This Team Charter isn't a legal contract or agreement. In fact, for some teams it may not even exist on paper. But, nevertheless, it is important. This is because it identifies the why, what, when and how of the team. It will provide the answers to questions like 'What are we going to do?', 'How long will it take?' and 'Who are our customers?' It will also answer the more subtle – but just as important – questions such as 'How are we going to work together?', 'Will we all be involved in key decisions?' and 'What principles are important to us as a team?' The answers to these and other questions make up the Team Charter. They need to be hammered out and agreed in this first meeting. It does help if somebody – usually the team co-ordinator – has thought through what the key issues are and prepared a draft document for discussion. This should tell the team about:

- its task – what, by when, at what cost, etc.
- its key customers – names, roles, expectations
- its task or project stakeholders – names, expectations, conflicts.

It should also give them some idea of the options for:

- how communications are to be managed – with and between customers and team members
- how team performance will be measured – key results, milestones, outcomes
- procedures and rules – must-be-done rules, areas of discretion
- how the team will work together – principles behind this team's operations.

The level of detail in this draft is important – too much and real discussion will be pre-empted; too little and discussions will produce 'broad-brush' generalities. It's also worth including in this draft statements that define the core principles regarding the way in which the team will operate. Examples might include:

- 'Working together is more productive than working apart.'
- 'Joint decisions are stronger than solo ones.'
- 'Team meetings are jointly owned.'

In the end, the content, detail, form and structure of the Team Charter is down to the team. But if it's going to work then it must provide urgency and direction to the team's efforts as well as being a means of focusing the creativity and energy of all team members. But that's not all that happens in this first meeting – for it's there that the process of team building begins.

Team building

Your team won't spring spontaneously into existence at that first meeting. It takes time for the team to complete the journey from being a collection of individuals to becoming a cohesive, supportive, flexible and productive team. This is a journey that'll take them from the inhibited watchfulness of their first meetings, through conflict and the development of their own 'home-grown' set of rules and standards to, finally, becoming a team. One of the more accessible views about how this happens tells us that a team 'grows' through four stages called 'forming', 'storming', 'norming' and 'performing' – as you'll see in Figure 9.1.

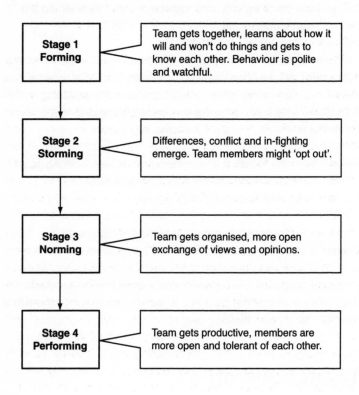

Figure 9.1: Steps and stages of team development

But the route that each team follows on this journey will be unique to that team. It has to be – since that team itself is unique.

Nevertheless, there are two key basic factors that are common to all teams. The first of these is about the importance spending time together. A lot of what happens in the team-building process is linked to the process of getting to know each other, getting to know and respect each other's strengths and weaknesses and finding ways of working together. This is a 'do-it-as-we-go' process that happens more quickly when people work in close proximity to each other. Walls and doors get in the way and it will need a dedicated team space for it to happen.

The second of these key factors for team building is in the way that conflict is handled in the team. But first, let's be clear about conflict. Conflict is necessary to the process of becoming a real team. It will occur because people don't get on with each other, because people have different attitudes or sets of values and because people have different expectations. But most of all, in real teams, it occurs because all of the team are committed to doing their best for the team. Dealing with it isn't always easy; often feelings run high and voices are raised. But dealing with it is a must. If you sit on it, ignore it, push it under the surface of day-to-day relations, then it'll just resurface elsewhere – and be the worse for it!

If you're going to deal with conflict effectively then you may have to change the way that you think about it. It has to become a constructive opportunity rather than something to be endured. The key factors in dealing with conflict are communication, communication and communication. Frank, open talking and real listening are 'must-do's'. These are risky. But they are essential if you're going to have a real team. Taking the risk to be open in conflict can, on the downside, lead to hurt feelings, hostility, enmity – even hatred. The upside, though, is the hard-won mutual trust and interdependence that's essential to a real team.

Good teams, bad teams

There are times and places when the team, despite its considerable potential, just doesn't work. This often happens when the team idea is misapplied or used inappropriately, resulting in disruption and wasted time and money. Teams can also come 'unstuck' because they are badly managed – resulting in the suppression or exploitation of team members' initiatives or creativity. More rarely, a team can become so locked into what it's doing that it begins to lose touch with the real world. What happens then is that it creates its own set of values and ways of seeing the world, leading to outcomes that are not compatible with or desired by the real world outside.

Another view of why teams fail says that this happens because the team:

- hasn't created an environment in which trust is important
- doesn't handle conflict constructively
- doesn't get commitment from team members
- avoids individual accountability
- doesn't have or create credible team goals.

When you think about these you'll soon realise how important effective communication is to your team. For almost all of these causes of failure will follow through when your team doesn't establish a commitment to effective open and honest communication – and as a result doesn't complete the forming–storming–norming–performing cycle.

But, despite all this, a good team with potential is worth the risk. For when it works, it's capable of moving mountains. Use the questionnaire in Table 9.2 to check out your team.

Table 9.2: Team Performance Questionnaire

Start off by thinking about your team and try to identify how well it is (or isn't) doing. Asking yourself questions such as 'How does it set its goals and targets?', 'How does it handle failure and conflict?' and 'What is its communication like?' will help. When you're ready pick the answer to each of the following questions that fits the way that your team operates. Then add up your points and take a look at the key below.

1. Communication
- The team always shares information, facts, data and feelings: **5 points**
- We share stuff when we've got time: **2 points**
- Nobody shares anything: **0 points**

2. Conflict
- When conflict happens we talk – openly, frankly and clearly – and get it sorted out: **5 points**
- We try to avoid conflict but when it happens the team leader sorts it out: **2 points**
- We don't have conflicts: **0 points**

3. Goals and targets
- As a team we all understand and agree what we will do and how and when we will do it: **5 points**
- The team leader usually talks to most of us about goals and targets: **3 points**
- Goals and targets are either individual or set from outside the team: **0 points**

4. Co-operation and collaboration
- We co-operate and collaborate with each other: **5 points**
- There are one or two groups that seem to work well together: **2 points**
- You have to watch your back around here: **0 points**

Table 9.2: *Continued*

---

5. Tolerance and trust
- We tolerate and trust each other: **5 points**
- Most of us get on well together and have
  learnt to tolerate and trust each other: **3 points**
- No way!   **0 points**

Key

Check out how you score:

25–21: Your team is working well!

20–16: You can probably work through any team issues and remain largely effective.

15–9: Your team can get its work done, but you have some significant issues to overcome!

8–0: This is not a team.

How did your team score?

Summary

In this chapter you saw that groups are different to crowds because the people in them have shared and sometimes interconnected objectives and do things together to achieve those objectives. These groups can also be formal or informal. A team is a special sort of group. It has:

- a facilitator/coach/co-ordinator rather than a leader
- goals that are set by its members rather than the parent organisation
- communication patterns that flow up *and* down, and

- members that:
  - make decisions together
  - work together co-operatively
  - are jointly responsible for outcomes.

A team like this has the potential to make a significant difference to the performance of your workplace because it make things happen and works in ways that out-perform the sum of individual efforts of its members. It should have between six and eight members who have been selected to work in the team because of their functional skills, their ability to work co-operatively with others and their ability to carry out the required team roles. The process of building a team will start with the generation of a joint Team Charter and continues when the team spends time together and finds ways of handling conflict constructively. This process can be said to have four stages during which the team:

- forms
- storms
- norms, and then
- performs.

Despite all its potential the team idea doesn't always work. This happens when it's misapplied or used inappropriately, badly managed, loses touch with reality, or doesn't support effective and open communication. Despite all this, a good team is worth the risk.

INSTANT TIP

When you are building your team try to remember that the letter 'I' doesn't appear in 'team work' – and for good reason.

10

What's your style?

Style is one of the most important ways by which you express your individuality. It can also exert a considerable influence on the quality and effectiveness of your workplace communication. This chapter looks at several ways in which style can be described and explores the influence that style exerts upon the success and effectiveness of those communications.

'Style' – what is it?

When you look the word 'style' up in your dictionary you'll find that it appears to be one of those 'portmanteau' words that brings together a number of disparate and different ideas. This means that it gets used a lot and in many different ways. The Oxford English Dictionary, for example, records some 28 different meanings for the word style when it's used as a noun. These range from a style being a *'stylus, pin, stalk'* through the more familiar version where style is a *'particular mode or fashion of costume'* to, at the end, style being a *'way of expressing dates'.* However, among all this variety, you will find three ideas about the meaning of style that will be useful to you when you explore its meaning in relation to your communications.

These tell you that a style can be:

'a manner of executing a task or performing an action or operation'

and, more specifically:

'a manner of discourse, or tone of speaking, adopted in addressing others or in ordinary conversation'

or:

'a writer's mode of expression considered in regard to clearness, effectiveness, beauty, and the like'.

All of these tell you that, when used in relation to communication, your style is the way that you 'do' communication or, to put it another way, the way you do what you do when you communicate with others. It's also, according to people who study these things, a collection or accumulation of 'micro-behaviours' that represent a relatively stable and long-lasting pattern of individual behaviour. But, as you know, the range of these behaviours is astonishingly wide. One of the ways that has been used to describe style has some nine ranges or 'spectra' of style – as, for example, in dominant/submissive or open/closed. These are shown in Table 10.1. When you look at these you'll soon realise that the style that you adopt in your communication will, to a degree, depend upon factors such as:

- where you're doing it
- with whom you're doing it
- what role you're carrying out when you do it.

Table 10.1: Style spectra

Dominant – Submissive

Dramatic – Reserved

Contentious – Affiliative

Animated – Inexpressive

Relaxed – Frenetic

Attentive – Inattentive

Impressive – Insignificant

Open – Closed

Friendly – Hostile

For example, a manager may adopt a dominant style when with his or her co-workers but may adopt a submissive style during the board meetings that he or she has been asked to attend. Nevertheless it's been observed by researchers that some elements of your individual style will persist wherever you are and whatever you are doing.

I'll do it my way

The style that you choose to adopt is a significant factor when it comes to both the manner and the effectiveness of your workplace communications. But it's only one element in many that make up the complex web that you weave when you interact with those about you. Because of this complexity, there are, as you'd expect, a number of theories about all of this.

Carl Jung – the founder of analytical psychology – developed one of the more accessible theories in the 1920s. Jung popularised the concepts of introversion and extroversion which tell you that extroverts, for example, tend to enjoy human interactions and to be enthusiastic, talkative, assertive and gregarious while introverts tend to be low-key, deliberate and relatively less engaged in social situations. But introversion is not the same as shyness. Introverts choose solitary activities by preference, rather than out of fear. These notions of how we behave now appear in virtually all ways used to describe personality including Cattell's 16 Personality Factors, the Minnesota Multiphasic Personality Inventory (MMPI) and the Myers-Briggs Type Indicator (MBTI). Jung also initially suggested that people could be categorised in terms of four main functions of consciousness; two of which (Sensation (S) and Intuition (I)) he described as perceiving functions while the other two (Thinking (T) and Feeling (F)) were described as judging functions. These functions are modified by the attitudes of extroversion and introversion and, in their most basic form, enable people to be described as:

- **ST individuals**: these combine sensation and thought and are often described as logical, arriving at conclusions on the basis of what they perceive to be 'hard' facts.
- **IT individuals**: these combine thought and intuition and are described as shaping their conclusions with ideas and insights – rather than facts – and as being concerned with the possibilities of a situation.
- **IF individuals**: people like this behave in ways that reflect the fact that their view of the world is strongly influenced by their intuition and feelings and can be described as being more concerned with values than facts.
- **SF individuals**: these combine sensing and feelings. They are primarily concerned with the evidence of their senses and arrive at conclusions on the basis of 'gut' feelings.

These basic 'people-pictures' were modified and extended in the 1940s by the American psychologists, Katherine Briggs and Isabel Briggs Myer, into a personality test that claims to tell you how a person prefers to work. This work resulted in a test – the Myers-Briggs Type Indicator – that identifies which of 16 possible psychological types you appear to fit into. These are based on following pairs of preferences:

Extroversion (E) – – – – Introversion (I)
Sensing (S) – – – – – – Intuition (N)
Thinking (T) – – – – – – Feeling (F)
Judging (J) – – – – – – Perceiving (P)

Other writers have annexed these into five basic managerial types whose outlines and associated Myers-Briggs acronyms are as follows:

Traditionalist (ISTJ, ISFJ, ESTJ, ESFJ)
Traditionalists or Sensing–Judging (SJ) types are described as practical managers who weigh up risks and consequences before taking a decision and are keen on order. They are said to be very good at handling data and co-ordinating but are not good with change.

Troubleshooter (ISTP, ESTP) and **Negotiator** (ISFP, ESFP)
Both of these Sensing–Perceiving (SP) types are problem solvers who are very flexible and able to live in the 'here and now'. They can appear unpredictable and disorganised.

Catalyst (INFJ, INFP, ENFP, ENFJ)
These Intuition–Feeling (NF) types are the communicators of the workplace. They care for people but may base their decisions on their values rather than facts.

Visionary (INTJ, INTP, ENTP, ENTJ)
These Intuition–Thinking (NT) types are the planners, innovators and creators of the workplace. They are good decision-makers but may need to be reminded about other people's problems.

While these basic types are said by some to oversimplify the choices that we all face as managers they do provide a framework of choice for the style that you adopt.

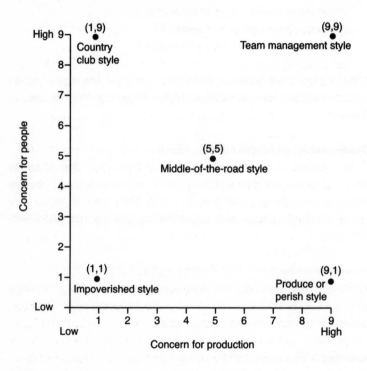

Figure 10.1: The Managerial Grid

Another way of looking at the styles that get used and adopted in the workplace is contained in the Managerial Grid Model (see Figure 10.1). This was developed in the 1960s by Robert Blake and Jane Mouton, uses the dimensions of 'concern for production' and 'concern for people', providing five basic views of the ways in which managers can and do operate:

- **Produce or perish style (9,1):** a manager with this style will use the skills of planning, scheduling and organising to keep the human factors to a minimum.
- **Team management style (9,9):** this style attempts to balance human and task needs.
- **Country club style (1,9):** this style has a high concern for people and a low concern for production. Managers using this style pay much attention to the security and comfort of the employees, in the hope that this will increase performance.
- **Impoverished style (1,1):** managers who use this style have low concern for both people and production. Often used to avoid getting into trouble or to try to stay in the same job for a long time.
- **Middle-of-the-road style (5,5):** this style tries to balance the goals of the organisation and the needs and wants of the workers.

But that isn't all that there is to style or the way that you do what you do. For psychiatrist Alfred Adler wrote about our individual 'styles of life', which he said reflected the individual's unique, unconscious and repetitive way of responding to (or avoiding) the main tasks of living: friendship, love and work. Style, he said, is what we are, who we are, what we want to be.

By now, it will be evident that style has considerable potential to influence the way in which you communicate in the workplace. So let's move on now to look, in more detail, at some of the views about the ways in which this influence – between style and communication – takes place. The views that you'll look at are:

● transactional analysis
● role theory
● assertiveness.

I'm OK – you're OK

Transactional analysis, or TA as it's often called, was created and developed by the American psychiatrist Eric Berne during the late 1950s. TA aims to describe how you and I are structured psychologically and uses what is called the 'ego-state' model or Parent-Adult-Child model to do this. It also uses this to make suggestions about the how and why of our communications.

Typically, TA tells us, we all have three ego-states that we consistently use. These are:

● **Parent**: an ego state in which we will behave, feel, and think in response to our memories of how our parents acted.
● **Adult**: an 'ideal' ego state in which we draw on all of the resources and experience of our lives as adult human beings and in so doing respond to what's happening in the 'here-and-now' rather than the remembered past or the 'might be' future. This is the ideal ego state that TA aims to strengthen.
● **Child**: an ego state in which we behave, feel and think in ways that are similar to our childhood patterns.

These ego states are different from actual adults, parents and children, and are described by using capital letters when describing them – as in Parent (P), Adult (A) and Child (C) – and within each ego states there are subdivisions. This means that when you go into your Parent ego state you can be either a nurturing Parent – as in giving permission and security – or a critical Parent – as when making negative comparisons to family traditions or ideals. Similarly, when you act in your Child ego state you'll behave in ways that are either natural and free or adaptive and reflecting the needs of others. These subdivisions tell you about the patterns of your behaviour, feelings and ways of thinking. They can be functional – that is positive and beneficial – or dysfunctional – that is counterproductive and negative.

As you've already seen, TA also talks about the ways in which we communicate. It uses the ideas of 'transactions' and 'strokes' to do that. Transactions represent the flow patterns of a communication, and occur simultaneously at both the overt and open level and the hidden or psychological level. Strokes are the recognition, attention or responses that you and the person you're communicating with give to each other. These strokes can be positive or negative. A key idea here is that we all seek recognition, and if we can't get positive strokes, we'll reach out for whatever kind we can get – even if it's negative. As a result, the transactions of your communication will be experienced as either positive or negative – depending on the sort of strokes within them. These transactions are important – even to the point where a negative transaction is felt to be better than no transaction – and can be portrayed as shown in Figure 10.2.

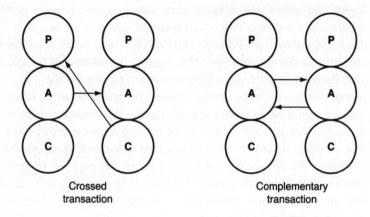

Crossed
transaction

Complementary
transaction

Figure 10.2: Transactions

Table 10.2 also summarises some of the things that get said and done in these transactions by each of the ego states.

When you look at Figure 10.2 you'll see that in a Complementary transaction the communication flow lines are parallel and reciprocal. A simple example of this kind of transaction would be:

Person A as Parent asks Person B as Child: 'Have you tidied your room yet?'

Person B as Child replies to Person A as Parent: 'Will you stop nagging me? I'll do it eventually!'

However, in a Crossed transaction, the communications are aimed at the ego state that the addressee thinks the other is in – rather than the ego state that they actually are in. Crossed transactions cause problems and a simple example of this sort of transaction would be:

Person A as Parent asks Person B who is thought to be in Child ego state: 'Have you tidied your room yet?'

Person B (in Adult ego state) replies to Person A's Adult ego state: 'I'm just going to do it, actually.'

Table 10.2: Ego state characteristics

Ego State	Words Used	Gestures Used
Parent	Always, never, should, shouldn't, don't, right, wrong	Pointing finger, arms folded across chest, sighing, patting another on head
Adult	Could, possible, true, probable, test, I think	Listening, continual movement of face, eyes and body
Child	Want, let's, wish, guess, dream, funny, magic, great, super	Whining voice, downcast eyes, teasing laughter, shrugging shoulders, asking permission to speak

TA also tells us that we each have a 'Script' and a 'Life Position'. Your script is the life plan that you chose for yourself in childhood and has a particular end-point or pay-off. Your script is often reinforced or confirmed by your parents and childhood experiences. In adult life, you will not be aware of its influence or contents. Nevertheless, it will influence how you see and communicate with the world around you. The same could be said of your life position. This draws strongly on your script and tells you about yourself and your relationship to others. There are said to be four basic life positions as follows:

1. I'm not OK – You're OK.
2. I'm not OK – You're not OK.

3. I'm OK – You're not OK.
4. I'm OK – You're OK.

TA says that, for most people, the 'I'm not OK – You're OK' life position – that is common in childhood – persists into their adult life. What TA aims to do is to provide the opportunity to change your life script and shift into the 'I'm OK – You're OK' life position. To do that TA aims to be goal-oriented rather than being just a problem-solving process. Its aims include freedom from your childhood script, spontaneity, intimacy, actively solving problems rather than avoiding them and learning about new choices. It also provides an analytical framework from which you can view and review your communications with others.

Role theory

If there's one thing that's not in short supply these days it's roles. For we all have lots and lots of roles. You, for example, could be a brother or sister, mother or father, son or daughter, boss, supervisor, co-worker, accountant, salesperson, social worker, etc. – the list of actual, possible and potential roles is endless. When you carry out a role you'll find that other people expect you to behave in a certain way. This 'certain way' of behaving consists of a set of behaviours that are relevant to the role you've taken on or been given. 'Relevant' means that they represent what other people expect you to do when you are in that role. For example, if you are the secretary of a voluntary organisation, you will be expected to do things such as take notes during meetings, contact other members regarding these meetings and other events, and keep track of whether people have or haven't paid their dues. But you won't do these things because of who you are but because they are the duties of the position.

But carrying out a role doesn't just involve behaviours. For the way that you carry out a role is just as significant and important as what you do. For example, if you were to carry out the role of a waiter or waitress in a restaurant, you would be expected – whether you felt like it or not – to be cheerful and interested. Fail to be cheerful or interested and you'll soon have the manager telling you how to treat customers 'properly'. So, the way that you do what you do – or the style of your doing it – is important when it comes to roles.

The style and ways and means of your communications when you are carrying out a role are, of course, a key element in these role expectations. For example, you wouldn't expect a minister of a religion to use bad or profane language nor would you expect a doctor to laugh when you told him or her about your ailment. These expectations about role communications can act to help you – as when people will see you as being an 'expert' on a particular subject because you've given a presentation about it – or hinder you – as when people don't expect you to express your feelings because that wouldn't be 'right' for the role you are carrying out.

Each of the roles that you carry out will have an associated 'role set' – a group of associated roles that are carried out by other people. Figure 10.3 shows a role set for the role of 'manager'. When you look at this role set what you'll see is that the roles in it cover a wide range of activities and expectations. For example, the expectations that a trade union official will have of the role of a manager will be different to the expectations that a customer has of that role.

In the end though, carrying out a role – any role – is often a complicated business. For not only are there the often remarkably detailed and complex expectations that go with that role, there's also often an enormous pressure for you to conform to or meet those expectations. Nevertheless, most of the time, we manage to meet those expectations and, as a result, these roles guide much of our lives, both in and out of the workplace.

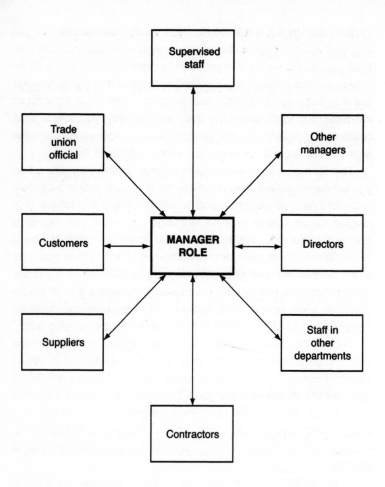

Figure 10.3: A role set

Assertiveness

If you look up the word 'assertion' in the dictionary what you'll first find is a definition that tells you that it is defined as *'the action of setting free, liberation'.* If you probe further you'll find that self-assertion is described as *'an insistence on a recognition of one's own rights or claims'*.

So what are all these about and how will they help your communication?

The answer lies in the fact that assertiveness is actually a way of behaving. As such you can't buy it in a bottle – it's something that you have to learn and to practise. When you do that – behave assertively – what you are doing is interacting with people while standing up for your rights. This puts assertion at the midpoint between the limits of two other sorts of behaviour – aggression and submission.

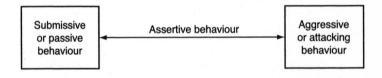

Figure 10.4: A spectrum of behaviours

These two extremes – submissive and aggressive behaviour – of the spectrum of behaviours shown in Figure 10.4 have quite different characteristics:

Submissive behaviour is generally exhibited by people who want to gain the approval of others and/or avoid hurting or upsetting anyone. They tend not to stand up for themselves or only express their views in a very cautious or mild manner. They say things like 'I'm sorry to take up your time but ...' or 'Would you be upset if we ...?'

Aggressive behaviour is generally exhibited by people who have little or no concern for other people and their ideas, feelings and needs. It often involves using sarcasm, adopting a patronising attitude or placing the blame for problems and mistakes on someone else. Agressive people say things like 'Don't ask questions – just do it ...', 'That's stupid' or 'It's nothing to do with me – it's all your fault.'

But when you look at assertive behaviour, you'll find that it's quite different to these extremes:

Assertive behaviour is generally exhibited by people who respect other people's right to express their ideas, feelings and needs, while also recognising that they too have the right to express their own ideas, feelings and needs.

Being assertive means:

- being honest with yourself and others
- having the ability to say directly what you want, need or feel – but not at the expense of others.

Assertive people develop the ability to negotiate and hence reach workable compromises with others. Doing this means having confidence in yourself and being positive while simultaneously understanding other people's points of view. Assertive people say things like: 'I believe that ... what do you think?', 'I would like to ...' and 'What can we do to resolve this problem?'

The differences, in body or non-verbal language, between passive, assertive and aggressive behaviours are shown in Table 10.3.

Being assertive is actually a social skill – one that's learnt. But it's also a skill that:

- is situation specific – in that its use depends upon the nature of both the situation and the interaction

- involves both verbal and non-verbal communication
- involves taking risks – in that it may not produce the desired result.

However, being assertive doesn't always get the results that you want. But what it does mean is that you become clear in your communications and, as a result, other people know how to deal with you.

Table 10.3: The behaviour spectrum characteristics

	Assertive	**Aggressive**	**Passive**
Posture	Upright, straight back	Leaning forward	Drawing away
Head	Firm but not rigid	Jutting chin	Head dropped down
Eyes	Direct with good and regular eye contact	Staring, often piercing or glaring	Little eye contact, lots of glancing away
Face	Expression fits with the words spoken	Set/firm	Smiling – even when upset
Voice	Well modulated to fit context	Loud or overloud and emphatic	Soft and hesitant, words trailing off at the end of sentence
Arms/ hands	Relaxed/ moving easily	Arm waving, finger pointing and jabbing	Still or aimless
Movement/ walking	Measured pace suitable to action	Slow and heavy or fast, deliberate, hard	Slow and hesitant or fast and jerky

At the end

The style that you adopt in your communications is, as you saw at the beginning of this chapter, an individual choice. It's a set of interwoven micro-behaviours that you alone have developed or adopted. You've done this for good reason – because you think or feel that this particular style results in successful communications with others. Being successful here means that it gets the results that you desire. As a result, there are no classifications of 'right' or 'wrong' when it comes to your individual style of communication. It either will do or won't do what you want it to and, in the end, that is what you must judge it by.

Summary

In this chapter you've taken a look at style and some of the views about the ways, means and outcomes of its influence on the way that you communicate. You've seen that style – in the context of both behaviour and communication – means the way that you do what you do. You've also seen that there some nine spectra of style and that the one that you adopt will depend, in part, upon:

- where you're doing it
- to whom or with whom you're doing it
- what role you're carrying out when you do it.

Among the many theories and methodologies that have been developed to describe the how and why of people behaviour you've seen outlines of those developed by Carl Jung, Katherine Briggs and Isabel Briggs Myer, and Robert Blake and Jane Mouton. You've also looked at three ways of describing the choices that you have when you communicate with others. These were transactional analysis, role theory and assertiveness.

INSTANT TIP

Your communication style is about knowing who you are, what you want to say or write, and then doing that briefly and clearly.

Index

Aggressive behaviour
   style, 191
Appearance
   body language, 52–54
Assertiveness
   style, 190–193
Attending
   listening, 30

Bargaining zone
   negotiation, 87–88
Belbin Team Roles
   team selection, 167
Blogs
   connectivity, 142–143
Blue-jacking/Blue-casting
   connectivity, 152–153
Body language
   appearance, 52–54
   bodily contact, 49–50
   facial expressions, 47–48
   gaze, 48–49
   gestures
      emblems, 46
      illustrators, 46–47
      introduction, 46
      regulators, 47

introduction, 41–44
methods of communication, 17
posture, 51–52
practical tips, 54–56
presentations
   movements, 111
   posture, 108
science, 44–45
summary, 56–57
use of space, 50–51

Clarity
   written word, 129–132
Clothing
   body language, 53
Communication
   benefits, 3
   communication channels, 8–11
   definition, 3–6
   difficulties, 17–19
   effective communication, 11
   introduction, 1–3
   methods, 5–6
   noise, 10–11
   one-way/two-way
      communication, 6–8
   summary, 19–20

Communication channels
generally, 8–11
Compatibility
persuasion, 72–73
Conflict
see also **Negotiation**
definition, 79
resolution, 80–81
teams, 171
Connectivity
blogs, 142–143
Blue-jacking/Blue-casting, 152–153
email, 138–141
future developments, 154–155
instant messaging, 150
internet forums, 141–142
internet, 136–137
introduction, 135
mobile phones, 151–152
online advertising, 153–154
podcasting, 143–144
social networking sites, 145–146
summary, 155
technological developments, 135–136
text messaging, 151–152
video conferencing, 148–149
viral marketing, 149
virtual worlds, 147
Voice over Internet Protocol, 148
Web 2.0, 154–155
web conferencing, 149–150
wikis, 144–145
Conversations
listening, 35
Crowds
teams, 158–159

Debate
listening, 36
Decoding
communication channels, 9
Dialogue
listening, 36–37
Difficulties in communication
generally, 17–19
Discussions
listening, 35
Dress
body language, 53

Ego State Model
transactional analysis, 184–188
Email
connectivity, 138–141
Emblems
gestures, 46
Encoding
communication channels, 8–9
Executive teams
team types, 163
Explaining
definition, 97–98
introduction, 95–97
methods, 98
presentations
audience, 105
audience contact, 107
body
movements, 111
body posture, 108
closings, 107
conclusions, 111–112
content, 104–105
equipment, 109
introduction, 103–104
openings, 106–107

practical tips, 106
preparation, 108–109
reasons, 104
speech, 110
visual aids, 109
spoken word
formal meetings, 100–101
introduction, 99
telephone calls, 99–100
summary, 112–113
written word, 102–103

Facial expressions
body language, 47–48
Feedback
degrees of feedback, 7–8
Filters
listening, 26
Flesch index
readability, 129–132
FOG index
readability, 129–132
Following
listening, 31
Front-line teams
team types, 163
Full communication
definition, 7–8

Gaze
body language, 48–49
Gestures
emblems, 46
illustrators, 46–47
introduction, 46
regulators, 47
Goals and glory
persuasion, 72
Golden rules
how
body language, 17

introduction, 15
spoken word, 15–16
written word, 16–17
introduction, 11–12
what
influencing, 14
information giving, 14
information seeking, 14–15
instructing, 13
introduction, 12–13
who, 12
Groups
generally, 159–161
teams compared, 161–162

Hearing
see **Listening**

Illustrators
gestures, 46–47
Individuality
style, 179, 194
Influence spectrum
persuasion, 60–62
Influencing
content of communication,
14
Information
giving, 14
seeking, 14–15
Instant messaging
connectivity, 150
Instructing
content of communication,
13
Internet
see also **Connectivity**
forums, 141–142
generally, 136–137

Listening
conversations, 35
debate, 36
dialogue, 36–37
discussions, 35
effective listening
attending, 30
following, 31
good hearing, 27–29
reflecting, 32–33
filters, 26
guide to good listening, 34
hearing distinguished, 23–26
hearing process, 21–23
introduction, 21
pretending to listen, 25
purpose, 26–27
self-evaluation questionnaire, 37–38
summary, 38–39
types of interaction, 33–37

Managerial Grid Model
personality types, 182–183
Meetings
explaining, 100–101
Microblogs
connectivity, 142
Mobile phones
connectivity, 151–152
Money
persuasion, 71
Myers-Briggs Type Indicator (MBTI)
personality types, 181–182

Negotiation
bargaining zone, 87–88
behaviour to avoid, 88–91
behaviour to use, 91–92

conflict, 79
conflict resolution, 80–81
definition, 81–82
introduction, 77–79
preparation, 82–84
stages, 85–87
strategy and tactics, 84–85
summary, 93
Noise
obstacles to good communication, 10–11
Non-verbal communication
see **Body language**

One-way communication
definition, 6–8
Online advertising
connectivity, 153–154
Organisational persuasion
generally, 69–71

Parent-Adult-Child Model
transactional analysis, 184–188
Partial communication
definition, 7
Personal space
body language, 50–51
Personality types
style, 180–184
Persuasion
compatibility, 72–73
fundamental aspects, 63–64
goals and glory, 72
influence spectrum, 60–62
introduction, 59–60
methods, 66–69
money, 71
organisational persuasion, 69–71
persuasive overtures, 66

persuasive situations, 64–65
self-evaluation
  questionnaire, 75
summary, 73–74
types, 62–63
Podcasting
connectivity, 143–144
Posture
body language, 51–52
presentations, 108
Presentations
audience, 105
audience contact, 107
body movements, 111
body posture, 108
closings, 107
conclusions, 111–112
content, 104–105
equipment, 109
introduction, 103–104
openings, 106–107
practical tips, 106
preparation, 108–109
reasons, 104
speech, 110
visual aids, 109
Project teams
team types, 163
PSK index
readability, 130
Punctuation
written word, 128–129
Readability
written word, 129–132
Reflecting
listening, 32–33
Regulators
gestures, 47
Revision
written word, 126–127

Role theory
style, 188–191
SMOG index
readability, 129–132
SMS messaging
connectivity, 151–152
Social networking sites
connectivity, 145–146
Space
body language, 50–51
Spam
email, 139
Spoken word
see also **Presentations**
explaining
  formal meetings, 100–101
  introduction, 99
  telephone calls, 99–100
methods of communication,
  15–16
written word compared,
  117–119
Sticht index
readability, 130
Style
assertiveness, 190–193
definition, 177–179
individuality, 179, 194
introduction, 177
personality types, 180–184
role theory, 188–191
spectra, 178–179
summary, 194–195
transactional analysis,
  184–188
Submissive behaviour
style, 191

Teams
communication, 168–169
creation, 164
crowds, 158–159
executive teams, 163
front-line teams, 163
groups
generally, 159–161
teams compared, 161–162
introduction, 157–158
performance, 172–174
project teams, 163
purpose, 162–163
selection, 165–167
size, 165
summary, 174–175
team building, 169–171
team charter, 168–169
Telephone calls
explaining, 99–100
Text messaging
connectivity, 151–152
Touching
body language, 49–50
Transactional analysis
style, 184–188
Two-way communication
definition, 6–8

Video conferencing
connectivity, 148–149
Viral marketing
connectivity, 149
Virtual worlds
connectivity, 147
Voice over Internet Protocol (VoIP)
connectivity, 148

Web 2.0
connectivity, 154–155
Web conferencing
connectivity, 149–150
Webcasts
connectivity, 149–150
Webinars
connectivity, 149–150
Wikis
connectivity, 144–145
Written word
clarity, 129–132
explaining, 102–103
generating text, 126
introduction, 115–117
methods, 120–121
methods of communication, 16–17
planning
information, 125
introduction, 121
nature of text, 123–124
purpose of text, 122
readers, 122–123
punctuation, 128–129
purpose, 120
readability, 129–132
revision, 126–127
spoken word compared, 117–119
style, 127–128
summary, 132–133
types, 119–120